JESÚS GONZÁLEZ ORTEGA
AND
MEXICAN NATIONAL POLITICS

BY

IVIE E. CADENHEAD, JR.

D1096950

THE TEXAS CHRISTIAN UNIVERSITY PRESS

TEXAS CHRISTIAN UNIVERSITY MONOGRAPHS · IN HISTORY AND CULTURE · No. 9 1972

Library of Congress Catalogue Card No. 73-161482
Manufactured in the United States of America

TABLE OF CONTENTS

*Editor of the Monograph Series
in History and Culture:*
DONALD E. WORCESTER

Front cover: The Mexican National Flag with emblem. Courtesy
of Mr. Juan Ch. Guerrero, Acting Mexican Consul in Fort Worth.

Preface

On Christmas Day, 1860, Jesús González Ortega entered Mexico City at the head of a victorious army. This event marked the end of a three-year period of disastrous civil strife known in Mexican history as the War of the Reform.

The war was the climax of a long struggle in Mexico, a struggle which had its roots in Spanish colonial times. Independence had not altered the old social and economic order. Except for abortive attempts to establish liberal programs in 1833 and the 1840's the Conservative Party, representing especially the privileged clerical and military groups, remained in power. Santa Anna, who had been in and out of power many times, took over as a Conservative ruler in 1853. His tyrannical rule led to a Liberal revolt in 1854. The success of this revolution enabled the Liberals to keep control of the capital and public power for two years. In December, 1857, the disaffection of the Liberal president gave the Conservatives the opportunity for which they had been waiting and a counter-revolution was begun. By the time the lines of battle were drawn, it was apparent that a full-scale civil war was in progress. This was the War of the Reform.

González Ortega, who had risen from obscurity in Zacatecas, joined the Liberal revolt against Santa Anna and emerged as an important military and political figure. The French intervention and Maximilian's Empire gave him an opportunity to add new laurels to his military record, but a constitutional argument with the republican president, Benito Juárez, added to previous disagreements, brought an end to his public life. He died in 1881 a bitter and disillusioned man.

Mexican history during González Ortega's mature life might well be compared to a three-ring circus, and, while he was not always in the center ring, it is necessary to watch the acts in the side rings to get a clear picture of events. This study is an attempt to review González Ortega's life and establish the relationship of his activities to Mexican history. Many important events have been treated only briefly or omitted altogether, especially where they have no direct bearing on his career. At the same time it is hoped that some new facts and interpretations have been contributed to an understanding of this period of Mexican history.

Work on this study was begun in the summer of 1949 at the University of Missouri and has progressed in stops and starts since that date. For the completion of the undertaking the writer wishes to express his gratitude to Professor Walter V. Scholes. His notes on the Reform Period, which he very generously placed at my disposal, were invaluable, especially those taken at the Biblioteca Nacional in Mexico City. The libraries of the Universities of Missouri, Texas, and Tulsa were of great help. The Library of Congress gave excellent service in obtaining microfilm of Mexican newspapers. Mrs. Evelyn Washburn typed an excellent final copy. Finally, credit should be given to the *Hispanic American Historical Review* for permission to use material published in my article, "González Ortega and the Presidency of Mexico" (XXXII, No. 3, August, 1952).

Ivie E. Cadenhead, Jr.

The University of Tulsa
Tulsa, Oklahoma

I
Journalist and Politician

The Mexican War of the Reform brought forth both patri-
ots and political opportunists and elevated to national prominence
many who might otherwise have spent lives of quiet desperation
in the provinces. One such man who emerged from provincial
obscurity to national attention was Jesús González Ortega, a Zacatecan journalist and politician. In 1860 González Ortega led the
victorious Liberal armies into Mexico City and soon emerged as
an important figure in the Juárez government.

Little is known about his early life (historians even dispute
the date of his birth), but he was probably born on the hacienda
of San Mateo Valparaíso in the district of Fresnillo, Zacatecas, on
January 19, 1822. His parents were Laureano Filomeno González
and María Francisca Mateos Ortega. His father came from Monte
Escobedo, Zacatecas, and his mother from Morelia, Michoacán.[1]

Laureano Filomeno González appears to have been the
manager of an hacienda. At least he had an important enough
position to provide a good education for young Jesús. For a time
González Ortega studied at the Seminary in Guadalajara, but
financial difficulties forced him to leave school and seek his own
livelihood.[2]

After pursuing several occupations, González Ortega finally
secured a position as secretary to the Justice of the Peace in the
village of San Juan de Teúl. Here he began to study law under
his employer, but at the same time he developed three other
interests which were to dominate his life: women, poetry and
politics.

According to one of his contemporaries, González Ortega
applied himself to only two things in San Juan de Teúl — poetry
and women. The same writer even intimates that González
Ortega's love of glory and liberty stemmed from the fact that he
looked upon them as two women.[3] Although there are no indica-

tions that the amorous adventures continued, his interest in poetry should not be discounted as simply the passing fancy of a young man. He continued to write poetry throughout his lifetime. Some of his ballads were published in local newspapers, and later the periodicals of Mexico City reproduced several of them. One writer stated that his poetry was dominated by the "most fervent sentiment and the deepest tenderness."[4] Actually, González Ortega's poetry did not achieve any considerable degree of recognition at that time or later, but the sensitive nature indicated by this avocation may aid in understanding some of his later actions.

During the time that González Ortega served as secretary in San Juan de Teúl, he was about thirty years of age. At this point in his life, his political beliefs first became apparent. To understand fully the choices which were presented to him, it is necessary to review briefly the conflicting ideas that existed in Mexico at that time.

When Mexico achieved political independence from Spain in 1821, the old economic and social order remained as before. Class distinctions continued, and the army and clergy retained their privileges *(fueros.)*. During the next thirty years there were many *tumultos* but no genuine revolution, and the Mexicans became engaged in a long and bitter struggle between Conservative and Liberal politicians — between those who desired to continue the old social and economic order within a unitary or central framework of government and those who wished to reform the old order and install a federal system of government.

One of the most important factors in the contest was the Roman Catholic Church. Its enormous economic interests and its control of education, not to mention its spiritual hold on the people, made the Church dominant in the political, economic, and social life of the country, and churchmen naturally preferred to associate with the upper classes rather than the masses. When the special privileges which the Church had enjoyed since colonial times were threatened, clerical groups were quick to rise in protest in the name of religion. The army, which also feared the loss of its privileges, was usually allied with the Church. Joined with these two groups were the great landholders, who also wished to perpetuate the system under which they were prospering. These groups formed the basis of the Conservative or Centralist party while the Liberal or Federalist party appealed to numbers of the middle class who desired opportunities in politics, and to a growing Liberal faction composed of men of all classes who wished to subordinate the Church and the army to the civil authorities.[5]

For a few months in 1833-34 the Liberals, under Valentín Gómez Farías, gained control of the government and enacted an imposing series of reforms. Moving to abolish the Church *fueros,* the Liberal government made payment of tithes voluntary (at least in theory); retracted, without penalty, religious oaths; completely secularized education and suppressed the clerical University of Mexico; transferred the right of religious patronage to the states; and began secularization of Church property. In addition, new laws reduced the size of the army and deprived its officers of their *fueros.*

The mass of the people, apparently not realizing what the struggle was about, refused to support these liberal reforms. Instead, following the habits of a lifetime, they rallied around the clergy and military and brought an end to the incipient Liberal movement.[6] As a result, the Conservatives returned to power in 1834 and were not dislodged until 1846 when the war with the United States gave Gómez Farías and the Liberals an opportunity to regain control of the administration. An attempt to revive the earlier Liberal reform program by obtaining a loan based on the mortgage and sale of Church property met such violent opposition that the Liberals were soon forced out again.

Throughout these years of conflict the state of Zacatecas was generally found firmly entrenched on the Liberal side. Gómez Farías became active there soon after independence, and from that time on he was an important influence. From 1831 to 1835

3

Zacatecas openly espoused the cause of federalism to the point of actual conflict with the Conservatives. Even after 1835 the Zacatecas Liberals were a constant threat to complete Conservative control of the nation.[7]

From 1848 to 1852 moderate Liberals attempted to govern Mexico, but despite the apparent honesty and sincerity of the presidents during these years Mexico was on the verge of anarchy by the end of the period. Both extremes, Liberal and Conservative, were dissatisfied with the state of affairs. On the Liberal side were a growing number of important individuals such as Benito Juárez, governor of Oaxaca; Melchor Ocampo, governor of Michoacán; Santos Degollado, professor of law at Morelia; and Guillermo Prieto, poet and writer. These men, representing various classes of Mexican society, had adopted the principles of Liberal French philosophy and of the democracy of the United States. Feeling that Mexico could be saved from anarchy only by subordinating the Church and military to the state, they began to take steps to achieve these goals.

Alarmed by the growth of liberalism, the clergy and generals drew together and planned to establish either a military dictatorship or a monarchy under a European king. Their first need, however, was to seize power, and the logical choice to head such a movement was Antonio López de Santa Anna, who had dominated Mexican politics for the greater part of thirty years. Although Santa Anna had proved unreliable in the past, the Conservative leaders believed that he could be controlled.

In July, 1852, therefore, when hatmaker Colonel José María Blancarte pronounced against Governor Jesús López Portillo of Guadalajara, the supporters of Santa Anna seized the occasion to make their own move. Though originally a local affair, the *pronunciamiento* was given wider scope by Blancarte after he was flattered into it by the Conservatives. In a short time other Conservative leaders joined Blancarte and proclaimed the Plan of Hospicio in which Santa Anna was called upon to replace President Mariano Arista, who was accused of having infringed the laws.[8]

During this period of national turmoil, González Ortega seems to have lived quietly in San Juan de Teúl awaiting an opportunity to take a direct hand in political affairs. Already a dedicated Liberal, he bitterly opposed Santa Anna and the Plan of Hospicio. A few days after the *pronunciamiento,* he and José María Sánchez Román arrived at the village of Tlaltenango. Here they organized a group of local citizens and disarmed a small force of militia headed for Guadalajara to join Blancarte.[9] González Ortega's action was directly opposite that taken by the governor and legislature of Zacatecas, for they supported the Plan of Hospicio. González Ortega spoke out publicly against this action and incited the people of Tlaltenango to protest. Their effort failed, however. On January 19, 1853, Santa Anna took control of the national government, and two months later Ventura Mora, a Santanista, became governor of Zacatecas.

González Ortega's stand incurred the displeasure of the authorities of Zacatecas, and they ordered his arrest and execution. But his popularity with the large number of Liberals in Zacatecas enabled him to escape apprehension. In fact, it is doubtful that a serious attempt was made to capture him.[10]

During the period of Santa Anna's ascendancy, González Ortega evidently devoted himself almost entirely to literary pursuits. He corresponded on literary matters with such men as the writer and historian José M. Vigil, and he also continued to write poetry and articles for publication.[11]

On the national scene, meanwhile, the administration of Santa Anna was becoming more and more objectionable. Santa Anna quickly grasped the ample facilities which many of the Conservatives were so anxious to bestow upon the central government and its chief executive. He adjourned the state legislatures and made the governors directly responsible to the president. At the same time, most of the leading Liberals were forced to leave the country.[12]

In 1854 the death of Lucas Alamán, the ablest Conservative

statesman, left Santa Anna without a restraining influence. Once again he sought plunder and applause, and the government increasingly took on the trappings of monarchy. The dictator rapidly depleted the treasury and was unable to raise additional funds. Soon the lack of money caused the defection of many of the generals and bureaucrats while the Liberal opposition became stronger.[13] A revolution was in the making.

On March 1, 1854, a group met at the village of Ayutla in the state of Guerrero and formulated a plan to withdraw recognition from the Santanista government. The Plan of Ayutla was ratified on March 11. Adherents of the plan pledged that the army would be sustained. They also provided for the formulation of a provisional government, promised that a constituent congress would be convened when a majority of the states had accepted the resolution, and invited Juan Álvarez, Tomás Moreno and Nicolás Bravo to assume leadership of the insurgent forces.[14]

Santa Anna attempted to put down the rising opposition with the aid of ten million dollars obtained from the sale of the Mesilla Valley to the United States, but it was a losing battle. The eventual outcome of the revolutionary movement became more certain during the spring of 1855 when many of the northern leaders declared in favor of the Plan of Ayutla and threw their forces into the struggle against Santa Anna. In August, 1855, after two unsuccessful attempts to defeat the rebels, Santa Anna slipped out of Mexico City and announced his resignation. For a few weeks the country was in confusion, since the revolutionists were temporarily unable to agree on a leader.[15] Finally, the leading revolutionists met at Lagos and named Juan Álvarez as chief of the revolution. At Cuernavaca on October 4, 1855, he was declared interim president of the Republic.[16] On November 14 Álvarez rode into Mexico City, and a few days later his minister of justice, Benito Juárez, began the attack on the reactionary forces by decreeing the abolition of all special courts and removing civil jurisdiction from ecclesiastical and military tribunals.[17]

In the state of Zacatecas the triumph of the revolutionary

forces was completed on August 17, 1855, when Victoriano Zamora defeated the Santanista governor, Francisco G. Pavón. Zamora named Severo Cosío as his Secretary of State, and Cosío in turn appointed officials for the various districts.[18] At Tlaltenango, Jesús González Ortega became *jefe político* with instructions to correct the abuses left by the Santa Anna government and to reorganize the administration. In this position he had an opportunity to make contacts and political friends and at the same time to demonstrate his aptitude for administration. He seems to have been especially successful in conciliating those offended by the anticlerical position of the new government.[19]

There is some reason to believe that in accomplishing this conciliation González Ortega was not as strict in his enforcement of the anticlerical laws as Governor Zamora desired. On at least one occasion Zamora reminded him of a state restriction on the operation of missions in Zacatecas and called his attention to reports that the regulations were being violated in his district.[20]

Despite such reminders González Ortega enjoyed the confidence of Governor Zamora and other important figures in the state, and they kept him informed of political events in both state and nation. He worked closely with the state administration on a Liberal program to build roads and schools in Zacatecas. At the same time, as *jefe político* he had an excellent opportunity to enlarge his own personal political following by recommending friends for political positions.[21]

While González Ortega consolidated his political position in Tlaltenango, the Álvarez administration in Mexico City was opposed by both Conservatives and moderate Liberals. The discontent produced a revolutionary movement in Guanajuato led by Manuel Doblado. On December 11, 1855, Juan Álvarez publicly surrendered the presidency to Ignacio Comonfort.[22]

Comonfort, though representing the moderate wing of the Liberal party, continued the reform movement. On June 24, 1856, he issued the famous *Ley Lerdo* which prohibited all ecclesiastical and civil corporations from holding and administering real property. A second decree, promulgated on April 11, 1857, regulated the amount and collection of fees charged by the clergy for their services.[23]

Comonfort's next act was the formulation of an *estátuto orgánico* to serve as an instrument of government until a constitution could be written. This statute, issued on May 15, 1856, provided for centralization of governmental authority, but at the same time limited executive power. Ecclesiastics were barred from participation in popular elections; free private instruction was permitted; and provisions were made for a bill of rights, for the prohibition of slavery, for freedom from forced loans, and for prohibition of civil and political distinctions based on birth, origin, or race.[24]

The *estátuto orgánico* was not popular. It did not go far enough to satisfy the extreme Liberal group, while some governors and officials protested against the law because it deprived them of the unlimited powers which they had been exercising. Most of the governors accepted it, however, as preferable to the existing state of anarchy.[25]

Meanwhile a constitutional convention met and, after months of argument, completed the constitution in February, 1857. In this document the Plan of Ayutla was consummated. The Constitution of 1857 provided for a federal system of government with indirect election of the president, the legislature, and the members of the federal supreme court, the president of which was also to act as vice-president of the republic. The document also included an unusually full and explicit bill of rights, abolished the *fueros,* and prohibited corporate ownership of land. Although there was no explicit mention of Catholicism as the official religion, neither was there reference to religious freedom. The Convention hoped that it had made a constitution under which a dictatorship would be impossible, but later events were to prove otherwise.

González Ortega was a substitute deputy *(diputado suplente)* from Zacatecas to the constitutional convention of 1857, but other political interests kept him at home.[26] In addition to his duties as *jefe político,* he began to edit and publish several periodicals along with his friend, Juan F. Román. At one time or another he edited *El Pobre Diablo, La Sombra de García,* and *El Espectro,* all published at Tlaltenango. At least one, *La Sombra de García,* seems to have been published primarily to support candidates in the coming state and national elections.[27] Aside from purely political subjects the paper also carried discussions of aims generally voiced by other newspapers of the time. It was especially concerned with the need for protection of the frontiers and control of the Indians and with the need for the introduction of new crops into Zacatecas and general improvements in agriculture.[28]

In April, 1857, Zacatecan Governor Zamora wrote González Ortega advancing the presidential candidacy of Ignacio Comonfort and asking suggestions for candidates for both the national and state legislatures. González Ortega either suggested himself and Román as candidates for seats in the state legislature or arranged for someone else to do so, because within a week he received another letter from Zamora giving him the latest information on the coming elections and warning him to handle the clerical group with care.[29] *La Sombra de García* threw its support behind Comonfort for president, Juan B. Cevallos for president of the Supreme Court, and Zamora for governor of Zacatecas. The paper's candidates for the state congress from the district of Villanueva (of which Tlaltenango was the governmental seat) were González Ortega for *diputado propietario* and Román for *diputado suplente.*[30]

In an editorial of April 17, 1857, González Ortega stated that Comonfort should be elected not because of his past accomplishments but because he was "the only pilot who can direct the ship of state while political passions still roar . . . ." Comonfort had taken over, he continued, "when a rupture was effected between the *moderados* and *puros,*[31] the latter proving themselves too exacting; when the most vital interests of the privileged classes were threatened with extinction; when the separation of some states seemed imminent; and when gloomy forebodings of general anarchy were evident;" yet he had maintained stability.

González Ortega also pointed to Comonfort's opposition to the radical policies of Melchor Ocampo, Benito Juárez, and Guillermo Prieto.[32] This, he said, seemed at first to indicate that Comonfort might prove an obstacle to the progressive movement and to the attainment of the principles of Ayutla. The creation of the *estátuto orgánico* also appeared at first to be an attack on the same principles and the needs of the people. Later events, however, showed plainly the need for Comonfort's actions. Comonfort, the editorial concluded, was the only man who could "make possible the march of the Republic along the path of reforms and progress," the only man with the "influence and respectability to quiet the passions of the country."[33]

González Ortega's attitude indicates that he felt the need for a stable government in Mexico even though it meant that liberal reforms would be achieved more slowly. This stand clearly associated him with the *moderado* group of the period, a rather unusual fact in view of the hatred he was to inspire among Conservatives at a later date. His desire for governmental stability would influence his career much more seriously in years to come.

When the new Mexican constitution appeared, González Ortega defended it both in the columns of his paper and in public speeches. One of the first questions he took up was the much discussed Article 123. Under the provisions of this article the federal government had the right to interfere in matters of religious observance and external discipline insofar as the federal laws might designate. The lack of a definition of "external discipline" seemed to indicate that it was subject to any interpretation a particular government might make. González Ortega attempted to show that there was nothing in the article to cause alarm and that the government had no intention of interfering with strictly religious matters.[34]

In a speech at the village of Teúl, González Ortega not only sought to win support for the new constitution but espoused a philosophy which definitely placed him alongside other Mexican Liberals of the day. Noting that "the improvement of the human race is a social necessity," he then continued:

the backward steps which it must take on the ladder of its reforms and conquests under the influence of circumstances are accidental and transitory things; and the human race is more perfect according as it has greater liberty, it has less restrictions, it approaches more nearly the Natural State under the protection of a well understood civilization. The human race then will march along the way of these reforms, although the corpses that retrocession piles up obstruct it and though fanaticism scatters its ground with anathemas. Providence, which took from the waters of the Nile the lawmaker of the Hebrew people, who were conducted by him from the persecution of the Pharaohs to the promised land, will carry the cause of humanity to the peak of its prosperity. . . .

The Constitution, González Ortega stated, was the fruit of the Revolution of Ayutla, but it did not represent the attainment of all goals. "When the penalty of death remains abolished," he said, and "when there is an absolute liberty of conscience, which in turn will open the gates to European emigration. . .then we can say that the promises of the Revolution of Ayutla have been consummated." As to the anticlerical aspect of the Constitution, he asserted that it did not attack the doctrines of the church or the "eternal truths." All that the Constitution asked, he explained, was just what Christ himself had expressed when he said, "Render unto Caesar that which is Caesar's and unto God that which is God's." Christ had not asked for *fueros* or riches, González Ortega concluded, so there was no reason for the clericals of Mexico to expect them.[35]

Shortly before the elections González Ortega used the pages of *La Sombra de García* to pass on to his readers some advice with regard to political parties. He said that political parties resulted from the "heterogeneity of ideas, from the clash of opinions and from the diversity of political beliefs." He warned, however, that "those which really deserve this name always follow a program, always aim for the realization of an idea and always try to establish and bring to the fore a principle, although what one faction calls a principle may not be considered as a truth by the other faction." The danger of false or impractical parties should be avoided. "Be alert, then, in the coming elections," he advised, "in order that we can distinguish between true patriotism and simulated aspiration and in order that the word 'progress' may not become a chimera among us."[36]

González Ortega proved an effective campaigner. When the results of the election were known, Zamora had been elected Governor of Zacatecas and González Ortega and Roman had won seats in the state legislature. Having accomplished his principal objective, González Ortega ceased publication of *La Sombra de García.* He continued writing for other publications, however, including *El Guardia Nacional* in Zacatecas.[37]

The new constituent congress of Zacatecas was installed on September 16, 1857, and immediately set about framing a state constitution. There was very little disagreement. The completed document was short and set up a federal, republican form of government following the lines of the Federal Constitution of 1857.[38] The Constitution was approved on November 5, 1857. González Ortega signed it as the deputy from Villanueva.

Though not a major figure in the early days of the new Zacatecan legislature, González Ortega earned some reputation for himself. He proposed a law requiring that episcopal pastoral letters be approved by civil authorities before being read to the public. The law was a direct result of the Church's attacks upon the Federal Constitution and the *Ley Lerdo.* Whether or not it was passed is not clear, although it created a sensation by going farther than any federal legislation at that time. The only other piece of legislation with which González Ortega was directly connected was a bill setting up a National Guard. On this item, however, he was simply one of a number of deputies pushing for enactment of a measure which would provide adequate protection of persons and property to encourage immigration. The guard would also protect the state against the central government should the need arise.[39]

While González Ortega devoted himself to state politics, the clericals had declared an uncompromising war against the Federal Constitution. A national decree requiring all public officials to take an oath of obedience to the Constitution was met by a clerical threat to excommunicate all who did so. This was only part of the dangerous situation that Comonfort faced when he was declared constitutional president on November 21, 1857.[40] He wavered in the face of continual attacks but evidently hoped that some compromise would be reached. Finally, feeling the need for stronger authority than the new Constitution granted him, Comonfort asked for suspension of guarantees of civil liberty and a revision of the entire Constitution. Though Congress granted the president extraordinary powers, the military and clerical groups seized upon his desire for a stronger executive. On December 17, 1857, Félix Zuloaga, the general in command at Tacubaya, declared in favor of a Comonfort dictatorship and another constitutional convention. Comonfort hesitated while Zuloaga took possession of Mexico City, dissolved Congress, and arrested Juárez, who was the newly-elected president of the Supreme Court. On December 19 Comonfort accepted the Plan of Tacubaya and declared a state of siege, asserting that the military authority had assumed power in order to re-establish public order.[41]

Realizing that civil war could not be averted, Comonfort again reversed his position, released Juárez, and raised an army to recover control of the capital. The Liberals could not be so easily reconciled. They declared that Comonfort had broken his oath and was no longer president. Under the terms of the Constitution of 1857 the president of the Supreme Court, Benito Juárez, became the legal president of Mexico. Comonfort found himself without a party, and his army was soon wrecked by desertions. On

13

January 21, 1858, he left Mexico for exile in the United States. The following day a junta in Mexico City declared General Zuloaga president, and Conservative armies gathered to eliminate the Liberals. Meanwhile, Juárez escaped to Guanajuato, where he set up a constitutional government and called for support from the interior states.[42]

A new upheaval faced the people of Mexico, the War of the Reform. Once again an attempt had been made to destroy the power and political influence of the privileged classes. Once again the Church and the army refused to accept reform and change. It was the old story of the status quo as symbolized by the *fueros,* threatened by liberalism as represented by the Constitution of 1857.[43]

By the spring of 1857 the lines of battle were fairly well drawn. Conservatives controlled most of the capital and federal district and the states of Puebla, Tlaxcala, and parts of San Luis Potosí, while a Liberal-constitutionalist coalition dominated Querétaro, Guanajuato, Aguascalientes, Zacatecas, Jalisco, Colima, Michoacán, Veracruz, and Guerrero. The war evolved into a conflict of the states around the periphery against those of the center.[44]

Comonfort's coup d'etat brought immediate repercussions in Zacatecas. The state reassumed sovereignty, gave the executive extraordinary powers and set up a council of state composed of José M. Castro, Francisco Parra, and Jesús González Ortega. González Ortega very early had cast his lot with the Liberal cause in Mexico, and in Zacatecas he had established himself as a spokesman for that cause. By the time the actual conflict began he was one of the men called upon to lead his state. On December 24, 1857, the state congress was closed. The executive and council of state were instructed to oppose the coup d'etat. Zacatecas began raising an army, and joined the coalition of states loyal to Juárez.[45]

NOTES

1. José González Ortega, *El golpe de estado de Juárez* (México, 1941), p. 20 (hereinafter cited as *Golpe*). The author of this work, who is the grandson of Jesús González Ortega, points out that the birth date has been given by other writers as October 11, 1824, but he has in his possession a letter from his grandfather giving the correct date, and naming his godparents as Benito and Ignacia del Hoyo. *Ibid.*, p. 412. Hilarión Frías y Soto, *Apuntes biográficos del ciudadano - Jesús González Ortega* (México, 1861) p. 9, gives the incorrect date. This work was published anonymously, but is generally attributed to Frías y Soto. It will be cited hereafter as *Apuntes*. A note in the González Ortega Correspondence Typescripts, I (University of Texas) signed by Sabino Gallegos, Civil Registrar of Valparaíso, states that his office contains a record of the baptism of one José Brigado de Jesús, the three-day old son of D. Laureano González and Dona Francisca Ortega, on October 11, 1824. Godparents were B. D. Rafael Guerrero and Faustina Valera. While the coincidence seems unlikely, it would be equally unlikely for González Ortega not to have known his age and the names of his godparents.

2. Victoriano Salado Álvarez, *Episódios nacionales* (México, 1945, 14 vols.), VI, 170; *Diario de Avisos,* September 22, 1860; *Apuntes,* p. 9.

3. Salado Álvarez, *Episódios,*, VI, 171. This account describes González Ortega as a ladies' man who was not particular in choosing his companions.

4. *Apuntes,* p. 9. According to the priest, Domenech, who wrote on this period and obviously hated him, González Ortega was a boatman in his youth and later a thief and a jailbird. Cited in Carleton Beals, *Porfirio Díaz* (Philadelphia, 1932), p. 108. *Diario de Avisos,* September 22, 1860, agrees that he was imprisoned during this period, although the reason is not given.

5. Richard A. Johnson, *The Mexican Revolution of Ayutla, 1854-1855* (Rock Island, Illinois, 1939), p. 4; Wilfrid H. Callcott, *Church and State in Mexico, 1822-1857* (Durham, 1926), p. 4.

6. Callcott, *Church,* pp. 84-99, 182-195.

7. Elias Amador, *Bosquejo histórico de Zacatecas* (Zacatecas, 1943, 2 vols.), II, *passim.*

8. Hubert Howe Bancroft, *History of Mexico* (San Francisco, 1885, 6 vols.), V, 607-610; Amador, *Zacatecas,* II, 507; *Apuntes,* p. 9.

9. Amador, *Zacatecas,* II, 507-508; *Apuntes,* p. 10.

10. *Apuntes,* p. 10.

11. José M. Vigil to González Ortega, Guadalajara, December 31, 1854, and C. de la Cagiga to González Ortega, Mexico, April 29,

1854, in González Ortega Typescripts, I.
12. Johnson, *Ayutla,* pp. 16, 28-30.
13. Bancroft, *Mexico,* V, 628-649.
14. *El Archivo Mexicano: Collección de leyes, decretos, circulares, y otros documentos* (México, 1856, 6 vols.), I, 5-9, and Francisco Zarco, *Historia del congreso extraordinario constituyente de 1856 y 1857* (México, 1857, 2 vols.), I, 11-13, both contain the text of the Plan of Ayutla. The amendments to the original plan provided for modifications if and when the majority of the nation so expressed itself. The resolution was thenceforth known as the Plan de Ayutla reformado en Acapulco. *Archivo Mexicano,* I, 10-18; Zarco, *Historia del congreso,* I, 14-18.
15. A good discussion of the moves made by the Liberal leaders will be found in Johnson, *Ayutla,* pp. 100-110.
16. *Archivo Mexicano,* I, 57-59. The leaders who signed the agreement at Lagos with Comonfort were Antonio de Haro y Tamariz and Manuel Doblado.
17. This law, which was issued by Juárez and which bears his name was concerned with more than just *fueros.* It actually set up a new court system for Mexico. Walter V. Scholes, "Church and State at the Mexican Constitutional Convention, 1856-1857," *The Americas* (October, 1947), p. 154. Text in *Archivo Mexicano,* I, 164-196. A more complete account of the dictatorship of Santa Anna and the triumph of the Plan of Ayutla is in Bancroft, *Mexico,* V, Chapters 5 and 6.
18. *El Heraldo,* December 12, 1855. The *jefe político* was the chief administrative officer of a district.
19. Amador, *Zacatecas,*, II, 528; *Apuntes,* pp.10-11. See also Bernardo Fernández to González Ortega, Teúl, September 22, 1855, in González Ortega Typescripts, I. Salado Álvarez, Episódios, VI, 171, states that González Ortega served as secretary to Ignacio Méndez Mora, *jefe político* of Tlaltenango, and mainly through his influence became a deputy in the legislature. While González Ortega may well have served a time as secretary, he certainly was advanced to the position of *jefe* well before any service as a deputy. José M. S. Román to González Ortega, Tlaltenango, September 10, 1855, in González Ortega Typescripts, I, would indicate that Roman was at least partially responsible for González Ortega's appointment.

Cosío resigned as Secretary of State in October, 1855, but continued to support the Zamora government and urged González Ortega to work closely with Zamora. Severo Cosío to González Ortega, Fresnillo, November 2, 1855 in *ibid.*

20. Victoriano Zamora to González Ortega, Zacatecas, January 18, 1856, in *ibid.* These restrictions apparently applied to the operations of missions only, and did not represent an attempt to close monasteries in Zacatecas. Certainly this action did not bring the violent denunciation from Conservative sources that later anticlerical action in Zacatecas did.

21. S. Cosío to González Ortega, September 8, 1855 and V. Zamora to González Ortega, April 24, 1856 and December 8, 1855 as well as other letters from Zamora to González Ortega in *ibid.* It would appear that González Ortega's poetic inclinations were not entirely without political application because he was requested by Zamora to write a march or patriotic hymn celebrating the date of the defeat of the Santa Anna government in Zacatecas. Zamora to González Ortega, November 16, 1855, in *ibid.*

22. *Archivo Mexicano,* I, 129-131; Bancroft, *Mexico,* V, 670-671.

23. Manuel Dublán and José María Lozano, *Legislación Mexicana* (México, 1877, 10 vols.), VIII, 197-201, 431-432 (hereinafter cited as D y L, *Legislación*). The first of these measures was the law known as the *Ley Lerdo* after its author, Miguel Lerdo de Tejada, then Minister of the Treasury. A discussion of its purposes and effects will be found in J. Lloyd Mecham, *Church and State in Latin America* (Chapel Hill, 1934), pp. 432-435. The second law became known as the *Ley Iglesias* after José María Iglesias, Minister of Justice under Comonfort.

24. Text in *Archivo Mexicano,* II, 110-144, and D y L, *Legislación,* VIII, 169-181.

25. Callcott, *Church,* p. 278.

26. The text of the constitution appears in Zarco, *Historia del congreso,* II, 993-1016, and in *Archivo Mexicano,* III, 26-66. Felipe Buenrostro, *Historia del primero y segundo congresos constitucionales de la república mexicana* (México, 1874-1882, 9 vols.), I, 46, does not list him as a delegate, although *El Heraldo,* January 18 and February 8, 1856, does. See Walter V. Scholes, *Mexican Politics During the Juárez Regime* (Columbia, Missouri, 1957), pp. 10-20 for a concise explanation of the political theories at the convention and the position taken by the conservative opponents.

27. Amador, *Zacatecas,,* II, 528, 556; González Ortega, *Golpe,* p. 20; *Apuntes,* p. 11. See also *El Estandarte Nacional,* February 13, 1857 and *El Heraldo,* April 15, 1857.

28. May 1 and 30, 1857. Román evidently handled most of the agricultural articles for the paper. On some matters González Ortega and Román were not in agreement and each had an opportunity to

express his opinions in the paper. See for example the April 24 issue concerning Article 123 of the constitution.

29. Zamora to González Ortega, Zacatecas, April 6 and 14, 1857, in González Ortega Typescripts, I.

30. In these elections an alternate (*suplente*) deputy was elected to take the place of the regular (*propietario*) deputy when necessary.

31. The moderate Liberals and extreme Liberals were called respectively *moderados* and *puros.* The primary difference between them was the speed with which they wished the desired reforms to be brought about. The *moderados* were more content with attaining their goals bit by bit.

32. Ocampo was Minister of Relations; Prieto, Treasury; and Juárez, Justice and Ecclesiastical Affairs in the Álvarez Cabinet, while Comonfort served as Minister of War.

33. *La Sombra de García,* April 17, 1857.

34. *Ibid.,* April 24, 1857. See Callcott, *Church,* pp. 304-305, for a discussion of this article and its interpretations.

35. *La Sombra de García,* May 9, 1857.

36. May 1, 1857.

37. *El Heraldo,* June 4, 1857; González Ortega, *Golpe,* p. 20

38. *Apuntes,* p. 11; Amador, *Zacatecas,* II, 559. This document was based on a proposed constitution drawn up on September 7, 1857, by José M. Castro, Francisco Parra and Belanazarda. *El Siglo* XIX, October 6, 1857. It was probably altered very little by the legislature. González Ortega was evidently not strong enough politically at this point in his career to be placed on this committee.

39. *Apuntes,* p. 11.

40. D y L, *Legislación,* VIII, 650-651.

41. José M. Vigil, *La Reforma,* in Vicente Riva Palacio (ed.), *México a través de los siglos* (Barcelona, 1889, 5 vols.), V, 228, 264, 267. The Plan of Tacubaya called for: "(1) inviolability of church property and revenues and the re-establishment of former exactions; (2) re-establishment of the *fueros;* (3) censorship of the press; (4) the Roman Catholic religion as the sole and exclusive religion of Mexico; (5) immigrants to come only from Catholic countries; (6) overthrow of the Constitution of 1857 and the use of a dictatorship subservient to Church only; (7) a monarchy to be established if possible, and if not, a European protectorate; and (8) high tariff, internal duties, and the use of monopolies."Mecham, *Church,* p. 440.

42. Vigil, *La Reforma,* pp. 274-275, 285; D y L, *Legislación,* VIII, 653.

43. Callcott, *Church,* pp. 84-96; Edward M. Caldwell, "The War of 'La

Reforma' in Mexico, 1858-1861;'' unpublished Ph.D. thesis, University of Texas, 1935, pp. 1-7.
44. Caldwell, "La Reforma", pp. 121, 126.
45. This council of state was actually the permanent deputation of the state legislature, a group that functioned when the legislature was not in session. *El Siglo XIX,* January 7, 1858; Amador, *Zacatecas,* II, 561. González Ortega had earlier offered his services as military commander of the forces in his district in anticipation of trouble and by November, 1857, preparations were being made for a possible conflict. Zamora to González Ortega, Zacatecas, August 28 and November 18, 1857, in González Ortega Typescripts, I.

II
Governor and Anticleric

At the outset of the war, circumstances favored the Conservatives who could depend on able generals, well-disciplined armies, and the assistance of the Church which, despite the *Ley Lerdo,* had the wealth necessary to finance the Conservative cause. The Liberals depended, for the most part, on the raw undisciplined state militias and citizen-soldiers, lawyers, journalists, and the like. The tenacity of these men and their refusal to accept defeat would eventually bring the Liberals success, but these qualities required time to show results, and most of the early victories went to the Conservatives.[1]

On March 10, 1858, in the first full-scale engagement of the war, the Conservatives won a major victory at Salamanca, Guanajuato. Two days later the Liberal commander, Manuel Doblado, capitulated at Silao. After only a few days of fighting the Liberals thus found themselves deprived of the services of one of their most outstanding generals and the road to the interior of the Liberal states opened to Conservative armies.

Control of Zacatecas alternated between the opposing forces. Governor Zamora resigned his post on March 21 and was succeeded by José M. Castro. On April 19 the Conservatives occupied the city of Zacatecas. One week later Liberal forces from Nuevo León under Juan Zuazua recaptured the city. In September, 1858, a Liberal defeat at Ahualulco, San Luis Potosí, again placed Zacatecas in the path of the Conservative advance.[2]

When the Conservatives marched on Zacatecas Castro resigned as Governor. According to the state constitution the office fell to Francisco de la Parra, president of the legislature. After five days the new governor, unable to organize effective resistance to the approaching army, also resigned.[3] A council of citizens named Juan Manuel Eguran as provisional chief of military affairs in the state, while González Ortega presented himself to the council and

21

claimed the governorship. Whether his claim was completely legal would be difficult to say, but he was the only remaining member of the council of state following the resignations of Castro and Parra. According to the state constitution, the president of the council of state became governor in the absence of the elected governor, so it would appear that González Ortega legally inherited the governorship. The junta members did not dispute his claim, and in October, 1858, he became governor of Zacatecas.[4]

In the face of the advancing Conservative army, González Ortega immediately recognized Juárez as head of the national government and Santos Degollado as chief of military operations. He then removed the government of Zacatecas to the village of Tlaltenango and turned to the business of aiding the Liberal cause with men and supplies.[5]

On October 24, 1858, the army of Leonardo Márquez occupied Zacatecas. Meanwhile, González Ortega, at his new "capital" at Tlaltenango, began revising the state's administrative organization in an attempt to reduce expenditures and raise funds to pay the state's debts. He issued three decrees designed to restore order and increase revenues. The first provided for the immediate punishment of thieves who were found guilty by a jury, and also limited army officers in the seizure of horses and money from private citizens. The second required all who owned pious property (*capitales piadores*) to pay twenty per cent of this into the treasury to alleviate the numerous and heavy taxes on the villages. The third decree imposed severe penalties on Conservative supporters.[6]

González Ortega spent the last months of 1858 raising and equipping an army to repel the Conservatives who were raiding the villages of the state. In the first weeks of January, 1859, the Conservatives withdrew from Zacatecas, and he moved there with a small detachment of soldiers and artillery. He then sent the major portion of his army to join Santos Degollado in Michoacán. Degollado had suffered a series of defeats in Jalisco and Colima before retreating to Michoacán, and he was desperately in need of reinforcements.[7]

The troops had hardly left Zacatecas when Joaquín Miramón (brother of Conservative President Miguel Miramón) moved on Zacatecas with an army of 2,000 men. González Ortega, though warned by others of the impossibility of defending the town, went out to meet the Conservatives with a small and badly equipped army. After two days of fierce fighting, González Ortega's forces won a victory. Miramón retired to Aguascalientes, and González Ortega placed his newly-raised division under the command of Julián Quiroga, a Republican leader of Aguascalientes. Shortly thereafter still another Conservative force invaded Zacatecas. González Ortega, refusing to recall the divisions he had sent to Degollado and Quiroga, met the invaders with yet another hastily raised army of volunteers. He not only drove the enemy from Zacatecas but pursued them to Valparaíso where he decisively defeated them in a surprise attack.[8]

Shortly after González Ortega's victory, Manuel Doblado, who had surrendered at Silao, escaped to the interior, and Degollado named him general of Liberal forces in Guanajuato. Doblado called on González Ortega for both men and material. In May, 1859, they united to win the battle of Las Ánimas and take pesos from the Guanajuato treasury. The Conservatives quickly seized on this action as evidence of the bad character of the Liberal leaders. The Conservative press accused González Ortega, Zuazua, and Zaragoza of fighting among themselves like common thieves over the division of the spoils[9] and added that since part of the funds belonged to British subjects, a great deal of damage had been done to Mexico's reputation.[10]

The Liberal victories in Guanajuato did little to change the overall picture of military affairs in Mexico, for the Conservatives continued to win in the field. They captured San Luis Potosí, occupied Guadalajara and brought most of the Pacific coast under Conservative control. Such setbacks did not mean the end of Liberal operations in those areas, however. Even though the Conservatives held the towns, the countryside was often in the hands of Liberal guerrilla bands which constantly threatened those in control.

The Conservatives faced other serious problems. Internal political troubles, coupled with the failure of a Conservative attack on the Juárez government in Veracruz, were climaxed by Degollado's siege of Mexico City. Although the Conservatives defeated Degollado at Tacubaya on April 10, 1859, and forced him to lift the siege, they gained an empty victory. In the aftermath of the battle the captured Liberal officers were shot along with a number of medical students who had gone out from the capital to care for the wounded. Degollado, who retreated to Michoacán and then Jalisco, retaliated by ordering that every captured Conservative officer be shot. Thereafter, the war was carried on with greater brutality and violence than before.[11]

The violence increased and its religious character was emphasized by González Ortega when, on June 16, he issued a decree against the clergy. In it he accused the priests of fomenting and sustaining the revolution to obtain more wealth and power. He attacked the Conservatives as hypocrites and savages. After this preamble the decree stated that crimes against public order would be punished by death. It also prescribed the death penalty for ecclesiastics who, before one or more witnesses, demanded a retraction of an oath to uphold the Constitution of 1857, or who refused to administer the sacraments because of such an oath. Equally guilty were those who served as witnesses at the retraction of the oath.

The law also decreed the death penalty for anyone who advocated destruction of the Juárez government or disobedience of its laws or its authorities. It was specifically stated that this last included sermons, pastoral letters, or any other documents read in the churches. In no case were orders from superiors to be considered as justifying disobedience of this decree.[12]

González Ortega's action was immediately attacked by the Conservatives. In view of his subsequent activities it accounts for the charges of extreme radicalism and anti-clericalism which Conservative writers made against González Ortega both at the time and later. One writer accused him of favoring a "baptism of blood" in order to bring about the reforms, while another writer charged that he was aiming for the de-Catholization of the country and the complete reduction of the clergy.[13]

Although the penalties prescribed by the June 16 laws were never carried out, González Ortega soon issued new edicts against the clergy which he did enforce.[14] He ordered suppression of all monasteries and the departure of all clericals, first from the city of Zacatecas and later from the entire state. In addition, other laws decreed the nationalization of clerical goods and legalized civil marriage.[15]

The González Ortega decrees forshadowed similar national laws issued by Juárez in July, 1859. The federal laws were motivated in part by the desire of the Liberal generals to seize Church treasures so that they could pay their own soldiers and also deprive the Conservatives of a valuable source of income. By these laws all ecclesiastical property except the actual Church buildings were to be confiscated.[16] Other laws suppressed the monasteries, declared the cemeteries state property, made the marriage ceremony a civil contract and recalled the Mexican legation to the Vatican.[17]

González Ortega immediately promulgated these laws in Zacatecas and took steps to enforce them.[18] He sent an armed force to Guadalupe to make certain that the banished priests departed. He authorized the seizure of a silver baptismal fountain and the copper bells of the parish church so that coins might be struck from the metal.[19] González Ortega was soon called the terror of the priests, for they feared that he would silence all the bells, convert their shrines into silver coins, and use all of the sacred statues for bivouac fires.[20]

His declarations and decrees also earned González Ortega the name of "Devil Preacher." Events in Zacatecas supplied the Conservatives with abundant material to paint a horrible picture of Liberal cruelty in general and that of González Ortega in particular. One incident reported in the *Diario de Avisos* is typical of the stories circulated about him. According to this report González Ortega appeared at a bull ring one day and before the fights began gave the bulls the names of the most venerable popes. The matadors were named after the leading bishops and archbishops in Mexico, and the picadors were given the names of the leading Conservative generals. When the fighting began, González Ortega shouted such things as, "Stick Pius IX, General Miramón. Now you, General Márquez, stick Benedict." To add to the disorder, the darts used to irritate the bulls were made in the form of tiaras, mitres, and calottes, and the stable guards were dressed in chalices, stoles, and other ecclesiastical garb.[21]

His own view of his actions González Ortega expressed in a letter to Pedro Ogazón in which he stated that he had not repented nor did he intend to repent his actions. To those who called him an enemy of Catholicism, he replied that for him all religions were good, even the Mohammedan, and "if I persecute the Catholic clergy, it is only to show them that they must obey, not in order to exterminate them, as my critics say." González Ortega continued by expressing his approval of a law of religious toleration, a law which "in my opinion, Comonfort did not issue in order to avoid an open break with border-line moderates and the enraged conservatives."[22]

During the last months of 1859 the Conservative victories continued. On November 5, Conservative forces occupied Oaxaca, and on November 13 Miramón defeated a Liberal army under Degollado and Doblado at La Estancia de las Vacas in Querétaro. This defeat not only put an end to Liberal plans to take Mexico City, but it was followed in late December by the battle of Tonila, Colima, where Miramón again defeated a Liberal coalition, this time under the command of Juan N. Rocha and Leandro Valle.[23]

Meanwhile González Ortega had remained in contact with Doblado and had supplied him with troops and materials — a drain on the resources of Zacatecas which left the city relatively undefended. In November the Conservative General Adrian Woll moved toward the city. González Ortega evacuated Zacatecas and retired toward Durango with Woll in pursuit. González Ortega managed to avoid capture and on his arrival in Durango he surprised and defeated a small Conservative force at Villa Nombre de Dios.[24]

Following this victory the Conservative press charged that González Ortega had ordered thirty-three prisoners shot and had executed eleven others during the march from Zacatecas to Durango. In Durango González Ortega was opposed by the local militia officers who objected to his interference in the affairs of their state and to an imposed contribution he demanded to sustain his Zacatecan forces. Fighting soon broke out between González Ortega's men and the local troops. When Colonel Miguel Cruz-Aedo, one of the Liberal leaders of Durango and a popular hero, attempted to restore order, he was killed and González Ortega and his lieutenant, Patoni, were held responsible. Opposition to González Ortega rose, and he retired from the city.[25]

Before his departure, however, he added to his notoriety by ordering an armed troop to remove silver and jewelry valued at over 180,000 pesos from the cathedral. The Conservative press again recounted González Ortega's "evil deeds" against the Church and against Mexico.[26] It would appear, in fact, that he had gained more importance as an enemy of the Conservatives than as a partisan of the Liberals.

In the state of Durango, González Ortega was joined by Governor Jesús Gómez of Aguascalientes, who gave him a number of men to strengthen his forces. González Ortega then turned back toward Zacatecas and, with the aid of General Trinidad García de la Cadena and Colonel José M. S. Román, recovered the city in the first week of January, 1860.[27] For this latest victory González Ortega received the congratulations of many of the Liberal chiefs. While his conquests had as yet achieved no major results, it was apparent that he was an able military leader who was making significant contributions to the Liberal cause. One

friend, Luciano de la Rosa, in a letter of congratulations to González Ortega, wrote: "You, my companion, like the immortal Washington, will be 'first in war, first in peace, and first in the hearts
of his countrymen'."[28] Even Juárez offered him aid and encouragement.[29]

González Ortega, during the first two years of the war, had
risen from the position of promising politician in Zacatecas to
governor of the state and leader of the Liberal forces in the area.
In addition, by his actions in enforcing the various anticlerical
laws, he had become — in the eyes of the Conservatives — one of
the leading representatives of all that was evil in the Liberal party.
Perhaps the major contribution which he made to the Liberal
cause during the first two years of the war was the raising of
armies and funds for other leaders. By the beginning of 1860 he
had also established himself as a capable military man,[30] although
it would be difficult to determine which contributed more to his
increasing fame, his military fortunes or the bad publicity he
received from the Conservative press.

Clearly an ambitious man — not only for himself but for
Mexico — and a man capable of inspiring others, González Ortega was now to turn his talents from political affairs to the waging
of war. Though trained as a literary man and adept at politics, he
was to gain his greatest glory as a general of the Liberal armies.
The former obscure poet and journalist from Zacatecas now
turned entirely to military affairs.

NOTES

1. Niceto de Zamacois in his *Historia de Méjico* (Barcelona, 1880, 18
   vols, with continuation by Francisco G. Cosmes published in 1901),
   XV, 296, states that of 61 major and minor encounters between the
   Liberals and the Conservatives during the first half of the war, the
   Liberals won only 16.
2. *El Siglo XIX,* April 2, 21, and May 3, 1858; *Apuntes,* p. 13.
3. Ignacio Álvarez, *Estudios sobre la historia general de México* (Za-

çatecas, 1877, 6 vols.), VI, 169, 175; *Apuntes,* p. 13.
4. Álvarez, *Estudios,* p. 176; *El Siglo XIX,* October 6, 1857. González Ortega, *Golpe,* p. 20, gives a slightly different version of this last change of governors. He states that Parra, in view of his other businesses, turned the administration of the state over to a junta. This was opposed by a group of deputies, among them González Ortega, and Parra was forced to resign. Then, according to this account, González Ortega was designated governor by the legislature. *Apuntes,* p. 13, merely states that González Ortega became governor following "legal procedure." *Diario de Avisos,* September 22, 1860, stated that González Ortega deceived Zamora and obtained the governorship.
5. Álvarez, *Estudios,* p. 176.
6. *Apuntes,* p. 15. González Ortega *Typescripts, I,* contains a number of letters concerning the enlistment of small groups of men and the dispatching of these troops to various locations.
7. *Apuntes,* pp. 15-16. See Manuel Cambre, *La guerra de tres años* (Guadalajara, 1892), pp. 132-198, for a complete account of Degollado's activities.
8. *Apuntes,* pp. 17-26.
9. *Diario de Avisos,* June 20, 1859.
10. *El Orden* of Querétaro, no date, cited in *ibid.,* June 1859. As late as July 22, 1859, the *Diario de Avisos* was still printing information on this subject. This particular issue shows the distribution which was made of the money among the various Liberal chiefs.
11. Bancroft, *Mexico,* V, 742-764; Cambre, *La guerra,* pp. 214-216, 235-247.
12. Vigil, *Reforma,* 376; Zamacois, *Historia de Méjico,* XV, 240-241. See also Agustín Rivera y Sanromán, *Anales mexicanos. La reforma y el segundo imperio* (México, 1904), p. 45. A similar proclamation had been issued by Degollado as Secretary of State and General-in-Chief of the Federal Army of November 4, 1858, but apparently needed this kind of state promulgation before any actions were taken under it. Santos Degollado Manuscripts, University of Texas.
13. Alejandro Villaseñor y Villaseñor, *Estudios históricos* (México, 1897-1906, 4 vols.) I, 136; Regis Planchet, *La cuestion religiosa en México o sea vida de Benito Juárez* (Rome, 1906), p. 137; Francisco Bulnes, *Juárez y las revoluciones de Ayutla y de reforma,* pp. 340-342; Manuel Valdés, *Memorias de la guerra de reforma* (México, 1913), p. 142.
14. Caldwell, "La Reforma," p. 170.
15. Villaseñor y Villaseñor, *Estudios,* I, 135-136; Rivera, *Anales,* p. 46;

Bulnes, *Juárez y las revoluciones,* pp. 337, 383. See also *Apuntes,* p. 24, and *Diario de Avisos,* August 8, 1859.

16. The Reform Laws were only one part of the general Liberal program, and the nationalization of church lands was much more than a revenue raising measure, but the immediate effects were to provide funds for Liberal armies and to change the status of the church. Scholes, *Mexican Politics,* Chapter 3, contains a complete discussion of the Liberal plans.

17. The text of each of these laws will be found in D y L, *Legislación,* VIII, as follows: nationalization of clerical goods, passed July 28, 680-688; civil marriage, July 23, 691-695; civil registration, July 28, 696-702; state control of cemeteries, July 31, 702-705; and recall of legation, August 3, 705, José Bravo Ugarte, *Historia de México* (México, 1944), III, 321-323, points out that the nationalization decree was caused by the need for funds and by pressure from Liberal governors such as Degollado, Viduarri, Ogazón, and González Ortega, who had anticipated this federal action in their states. Bulnes, *Juárez y las revoluciones,* p. 337, states that González Ortega followed Viduarri in the nationalization of clerical goods, but was the first to prohibit religious processions and to excloister the monks.

18. *Diario de Avisos,* August 8 and September 5, 1859.

19. Zamacois, *Historia de Méjico,* XV, 291; Rivera, *Anales,* p. 51. Planchet, *Cuestión,* p. 137, contains a violent denunciation of Gonzalez Ortega's actions. González Ortega to Pedro Ogazón, October 30, 1859, intercepted letter in *Diario de Avisos,* December 21, 1860, contains González Ortega's defense of his actions.

20. Justo Sierra, *Juárez su obra y su tiempo* (México, 1905-1906), p. 194. Caldwell, "La Reforma," pp. 52-64, concludes that the aid given the Conservative cause by the church forced the Liberals into such actions and that, in spite of this, the Conservatives still obtained more church wealth than the Liberals.

21. August 26, 1859.

22. González Ortega to Ogazón, October 30, 1859, intercepted letter in *Diario de Avisos,* December 21, 1860.

23. Rivera, *Anales,* pp. 48-49; Bancroft, *Mexico,* V, 771-773; Cambre, *La guerra,* pp. 416-417, 441-458.

24. González Ortega to Doblado, Zacatecas, August 24, 1859; Degollado to Doblado, San Luis Potosí, August 26, 1859, and González Ortega to Doblado, Zacatecas, Sept. 1, 1859, in Carlos E. Castañeda (ed.), "La guerra de reforma segun el archivo del Gral. D. Manuel Doblado, 1857-1860," in *Nuevos documentos inéditos o muy raros*

para la historia de México (San Antonio, 1930), pp. 82-83, 85-86, 93-94.

25. *Diario de Avisos,* January 17, 1860; Zamacois, *Historia de Méjico,* XV, 356; Antonio Gibaja y Patrón, *Comentario crítico, histórico, auténtico, a las revoluciones sociales de México* (México, 1934-1935, 5 vols.), IV, 310; Bulnes, *Juárez y las revoluciones,* p. 561. As will be seen González Ortega and his lieutenant, Patoni, were held responsible for the death of Cruz-Aedo by some of his friends. Valdés, *Memorias,* p. 214.

26. Rivera, *Anales,* p. 51; Planchet, *Cuestión,* p. 137; *Diario de Avisos,* January 29, 1860.

27. González Ortega, *Golpe,* p. 24; *Apuntes,* pp. 28-29.

28. Luciano de la Rosa to González Ortega, Pinos, January 10, 1860; Degollado to González Ortega, San Luis Potosí, November 17, 1859, and other letters in González Ortega Typescripts, I.

29. Juárez to González Ortega, Veracruz, December 28, 1859, in *ibid.*

30. Numerous letters during the fall and winter of 1859-1860 in González Ortega Typescripts, I, indicate the variety of aid given by González Ortega to others if not the exact extent of such aid.

III
Victorious General and Popular Hero

During the winter of 1859-1860 the tide began to turn slowly, almost imperceptibly, in favor of the Liberals. Miramón made a second attempt to capture Veracruz. The second siege began exactly one year after the first, lasted the same length of time, and fared no better. At the same time, activities in the interior increased and were advantageous to Juárez' generals.[1]

Changes in the Conservative high command also favored the Liberals. Silverio Ramírez replaced General Adrian Woll in Zacatecas, while Woll took charge of operations in Jalisco. Ramírez was not an able military man, and he lacked capable advisors. One writer even goes so far as to say that the fate of all Mexico was decided when Ramírez replaced Woll in Zacatecas.[2]

Early in 1860 González Ortega, who had turned entirely to military affairs, placed the executive authority of Zacatecas in the hands of his faithful supporter, Miguel Auza, and set out against the Conservative forces. Thereafter Auza and other loyal friends provided González Ortega with effective support, kept him fully informed and did everything possible to supply him with money, men, horses and other materials.[3]

González Ortega spent the month of February sparring with the forces of Ramírez in the area around Zacatecas and Fresnillo. Then, on March 16, six days before Miramón lifted the siege of Veracruz, Ramírez surprised and defeated González Ortega near Salinas in the state of San Luis Potosí. In this action, González Ortega lost a considerable number of men and a large amount of equipment, and his second-in-command, Sánchez Román, was killed.[4] The Conservatives then occupied Zacatecas while González Ortega retreated to Aguascalientes and Jalisco to reorganize his forces. On March 19, only three days after his defeat at Salinas, González Ortega attacked and took the town of Aguascalientes.[5] Early in April he was joined by the forces of José López Uraga, and together they retook the city of Zacatecas, forcing Ramírez to retire to Fresnillo. It would appear that this victory was brought about largely by the inability of Ramírez to organize an effective defense in Zacatecas after the battle of Salinas.

During the next few months González Ortega remained in Zacatecas, raising troops and gathering money and supplies. Uraga meanwhile led his command in search of the enemy. On April 24, Rómulo Díaz de la Vega attacked Uraga's forces at Loma Alta north of San Luis, but Uraga successfully threw back the advance and defeated and captured Díaz along with a large number of others.[6] Uraga turned his prisoners over to González Ortega, and although he was evidently acting independently, the *Diario de Avisos* reported the action as a victory for González Ortega.[7] Reports from San Luis Potosí and Zacatecas during this period showed an ever-increasing fear of González Ortega and respect for his military ability.[8]

During the next few weeks, González Ortega and Ramírez continued their sparring tactics, but fought no decisive battle. Around the middle of May, however, Ramírez won a victory in a minor engagement at Malapelan, and early in June was once again in control of the city of Zacatecas.[9]

On June 15, 1860, events reached a climax. González Ortega attacked Ramírez at the hacienda of Peñuelas in Aguascalientes and decisively defeated him. The action lasted only three hours, but whole battalions surrendered, and large amounts of ammunition and supplies fell into the victor's hands.[10] Although the full significance of the victory at Peñuelas probably was not evident to the Liberals at the time it has since become clear that this may well have been the turning point of the war and the beginning of the Liberal victory. The historian Justo Sierra expressed this belief as follows:

> It began in Peñuelas; Ortega, a journalist saturated to the marrow with revolutionary rhetoric, an orator of lofty phrases and doubtful eloquence, but brave, impetuous, full of

fervor and exaltation, occasionally a poet, profoundly sensual and gallant, but capable of acts of supreme energy on the field of battle and of supreme generosity on the field of victory; González Ortega, chief of the national guard, deputy and finally governor of Zacatecas, took in Peñuelas a conspicuous place in history. He, the enraged anti-clericist, the persecutor of priests, . . . the terror of the bishops, . . . not only vanquished General Ramírez, who came from Durango to reinforce Miramón, but also pardoned all the official prisoners, as if he obeyed some inspiration, as if he were occupied more with the future than the present, as if, with visions of crossing the Red Sea to arrive at a definite triumph, a warm moment of pity for the Fatherland had melted his poet's heart and was expected to disarm the hands of his adversaries, in order to make easier the embrace with which he could conclude this struggle.[11]

González Ortega's soldiers were certainly inspired by their victory and the confidence of their leader. When asked his plans after Peñuelas, González Ortega replied confidently that his only plan was to find Miramón wherever he was and destroy him. This kind of talk, even if exaggerated, gave encouragement and hope to his followers.[12] Many of the Liberal leaders joined Juárez in sending messages of congratulations in the weeks following the defeat of Ramírez. The eventual victory of the Liberal cause was clearly anticipated by this time.[13]

Following the victory at Peñuelas, González Ortega took a step which even the Conservatives found difficult to criticize. He proposed to General Miramón the exchange of Díaz de la Vega and other prisoners taken at Loma Alta for General Uraga and other Constitutionalist officers who had been recently captured at Guadalajara. Miramón rejected the proposal, but González Ortega, after reporting this refusal to the prisoners, set them free unconditionally. His action was indeed unusual in a war which had seen so much violence on both sides.[14]

The Conservative historian Zamacois admitted that González Ortega showed magnanimity and generosity with the conquered, but he added that this act only neutralized González Ortega's earlier action in Durango when he had ordered thirty-three prisoners shot.[15] The *Diario de Avisos* did not feel that the freeing of the prisoners atoned for the captives killed at Nombre de Dios and for all the other atrocities González Ortega had allegedly committed. The *Diario* argued that the Conservatives had freed prisoners hundreds of times, and that González Ortega must have had some ulterior although unknown motive.[16]

To discredit González Ortega further, another story of his misdeeds was circulated in connection with the victory of Peñuelas. According to this report he went to Salinas shortly after the battle and there heard that an official of the town, Ciro Alcain, had been in contact with General Ramírez just before a battle near that town in March. It was alleged that Alcain's information had enabled Ramírez to win a victory at Salinas. As a result of this allegation González Ortega dispatched troops to pick up Alcain and threaten to shoot him unless he paid 100,000 pesos. At first Alcain denied everything, but then offered to pay a smaller sum. He was taken to a ranch in Zacatecas and a firing squad was selected and set up in his presence. Alcain then offered 60,000 pesos, which was all he possessed, and González Ortega accepted. A month later Alcain was reported to be still suffering from shock.[17]

While González Ortega was engaged at Peñuelas, numerous indications of dissension began to appear in the Liberal ranks based partly on personal ambition and partly on political differences. In March and April, 1860, there was a definite move on the part of the northern Liberal leader Santiago Vidaurri — who had consistently resented government interference with his private domain — to set up a separate government composed of Zacatecas and Nuevo León.[18] Doblado, who favored the return of Comonfort and the moderate Liberals to power, seems to have considered such a plan for a time, although he had very little in common with Vidaurri outside of the personal desire for power.[19] Doblado approached González Ortega for an opinion on this subject, but he refused to participate in the plot, protesting his allegiance to the national government and his desire for nothing more than the victory of the Liberal cause.[20] This defense of legality and denial of personal ambition was characteristic of González Ortega throughout his public life. If it was nothing more than the pose of a self-seeking politician, he kept his true aims better concealed than most.

Whatever the cause of disagreement in Liberal ranks, it was submerged in the press of military matters. While General Miramón, who had defeated Uraga at Guadalajara in May, made preparations for a concerted effort to regain the ground the Conservatives had lost, González Ortega consolidated his forces at Lagos, Jalisco, and called for other Liberals to join him.[21] Zaragoza, Doblado, and Berriozábal soon joined him in the vicinity of Lagos, and on August 10 this Liberal coalition moved against Miramón in the Silao hills of Guanajuato. Once again González Ortega scored a military triumph. Decisively defeated, Miramón fled to Mexico City while the Liberals occupied Silao, Querétaro, Celaya, and Guanajuato.[22]

Following the victory at Silao, González Ortega repeated his performance at Loma Alta and Peñuelas by releasing all of the prisoners, and he even ordered the distribution of money to them. According to the Conservative historian, Luis G. Cuevas, this humanitarian act accounted in large measure for the final Liberal triumph. According to Cuevas: "the generosity and clemency exercised by the Liberal chief of the army during the last year of the war" swelled his army with disciplined and brave people.[23] Zacamois also points out that González Ortega did not win all his victories on the field of battle. In each town where he stopped he gave a ball and invited the principal families of the locality. He then directed his young officers to try to win the hearts of the local belles so that after his army departed there would be capable agents left to aid the Liberal cause.[24]

Once again letters of congratulation poured in to González Ortega, and on August 12, 1860, Degollado named him general-in-chief of the armies of the Center and the North.[25] In an address to his troops González Ortega thanked them for their victories and assured them with Biblical allusions that the walls of Mexico City would fall before them and the immense treasures there would be distributed to them. He told them that he, himself, was poor and that his poverty was the best guarantee that he desired the victory only for them.[26]

The Conservatives found it difficult to believe that defeat was so near. As a result of recent military successes, the entire republic, except for the cities of Guadalajara, Tepic, Mexico, and Puebla, was now under Liberal control.[27] Even when news was received in Mexico City that González Ortega was planning to move in that direction, there were many persons who refused to believe it.[28] The Conservative high command, however, recognized fully the danger of their position. González Ortega concentrated his forces at Querétaro in anticipation of a move against Mexico City. On August 20 he addressed a circular to the foreign ministers resident in the capital, advising them that he had orders to take the city by force, and that his government would not be responsible for injuries or damages suffered by foreign residents. This circular was also designed to encourage disloyalty to the Conservative government by the citizens in Mexico City, some of whom it was hoped might change sides with defeat imminent.[29] The Spanish minister, J. F. Pacheco, offered to mediate between González Ortega and Miramón, but the former brushed the offer aside.[30]

Despite González Ortega's announcement, the Liberal attack on Mexico City did not take place immediately. The Constitutional contingent from Tamaulipas was called away, and this had some influence in postponing the attack. Another reason for delay was the seasonal weather which rendered military operations in the Valley of Mexico impractical for a time. Even more important than these considerations was the presence of a strong

Conservative force at Guadalajara which Degollado thought should be destroyed before the march on the capital began. New plans were made with this objective in mind.[31]

Problems of military strategy were not the only ones facing the Liberals at this point. There was considerable personal rivalry among the more important Liberal leaders as well as among the lower ranking officers, and González Ortega was not immune to these jealousies. Doblado, for example, disputed the right to command in the attack on Guadalajara, but González Ortega's recent victories turned the balance in his favor.[32] Furthermore, various commanders serving under González Ortega were envious of his success and at the same time anxious to make certain that their troops received what they considered a fair division of any spoils the army might obtain. Typical, perhaps, of the attitude of the lesser officers was that of Felipe B. Berriozábal, who wrote to González Ortega complaining about the division of spoils after Silao. "Remember," Berriozábal warned, "that you are now not just a brigade chief in the division of Zacatecas, but General-in-chief of an army of operations and consequently you must protect all equally."[33]

González Ortega's own ambitions were still the subject of much speculation. The *Diario de Avisos* asserted in August, 1860, that his claim to be interested in the cause of the people, without any desires for himself, was nothing more than a pose, and that in reality he wanted to be president.[34] To back up this charge the paper published an alleged letter from González Ortega to Pablo Morales in which he stated "The presidency belongs to me by right,"[35] but whether he had serious designs on the office at this time or merely anticipated his election because of his military victories is difficult to ascertain.

Of more immediate consequence to the Liberal cause than González Ortega's possible presidential ambitions was an acute shortage of funds. With the sudden massing of large Liberal forces in the neighborhood of Mexico City the Liberals faced a grave financial crisis. González Ortega went to Guanajuato to seek aid, but money and supplies were so scarce that some other source had to be found. In desperation the Liberal Commander-in-Chief, Santos Degollado, suggested to him the possibility of seizing a *conducta* carrying silver from the British owned mines in the interior.[36] Before Degollado could act, however, Manuel Doblado ordered General Ignacio Echagaray to seize a *conducta* bound for Tampico at Laguna Seca near San Luis Potosí. Unfortunately, the silver train, worth more than a million pesos, was the property of British interests; and although Degollado assumed full responsibility, Doblado's action created an international incident.[37]

With the siege of Guadalajara under way and the Liberals on the verge of complete victory, Degollado became alarmed over the possibility of foreign intervention and succumbed to the vigorous policy of George W. Mathew, the British minister in Mexico. Degollado agreed to return $400,000 of the confiscated silver and proposed a plan of pacification with Mathew as the mediator. Degollado wrote to Mathew that he did not believe the country could be pacified by force of arms alone but only by mutual concessions, and that, although he favored the Liberal principles, he would be willing to compromise in the matter of the form of the institutions and the personnel of the government. He added that if his propositions were rejected by both parties he would retire from public affairs, but if rejected only by the Conservatives he would favor continuing the war. He proposed that a congress should meet within three months to decree a constitution on the basis of the reform laws, and that the diplomatic corps, together with representatives of the two rival parties, should name a president. The person so selected was to be neither Miramón nor Juárez.[38]

Degollado then wrote to Juárez informing him of the action that he had taken, and asserted that González Ortega was in accord with the expressed bases of the plan, and that Doblado would accept any decision of the government. He repeated his promise to resign if Juárez failed to accept this plan.[39] He sent the plan to González Ortega, who was then besieging Guadalajara, with the comment that the proposal conformed to the ideas they had expressed earlier in a conversation at Guanajuato. González Ortega called a meeting of Liberal chiefs to consider the proposal, and on September 30 they unanimously and vehemently rejected it.[40]

On October 4 Juárez notified Degollado and González Ortega of his rejection of the plan. He pointed out that the war was being fought not over the personality of the president but over questions of fundamental law. To González Ortega he expressed his faith in the state governors' continued support of the principles of legality. This support, Juárez explained, would guarantee future peace for the country.[41] The government, already embarassed by the seizure of the *conducta,* immediately removed Degollado from the command which he held only nominally, and ordered him to Veracruz.

While these events were taking place, González Ortega had advanced a similar transaction on his own account. As early as September 18 he had expressed his intention to try to bribe Severo Castillo, commander of the Conservative forces at Guadalajara, and if this failed to try to reach some peaceful agreement for the surrender of the town.[42] On September 22 he informed Castillo that he wished to meet with him and discuss the surrender. The meeting was arranged to take place at San Pedro for the evening of the next day, after González Ortega had advised Castillo that any agreement they might reach must have the approval of the Juárez government to be binding.[43]

At the meeting Castillo told González Ortega his conditions: the Constitution of 1857 must be reformed and Juárez must be removed from the presidency. González Ortega agreed to these terms because, as he explained in a later report to the government, these pretentions could be conciliated with constitutional principles. He felt that Juárez would step down if the reform program for the people of Mexico could be advanced by such a move. The revision of the constitution, he granted, must take place by a decree of the national congress, but this could be accomplished in accordance with the existing laws.[44] González Ortega's concessions evidently surprised Castillo, who then complained that someone just as bad as Juárez would become president. Castillo increased his demands, and the negotiations came to nothing.

Many persons, both at the time and later, considered González Ortega's actions as dishonorable as those of Degollado.[45] The only official censure which González Ortega received, however, was from Degollado, who reminded him that "neither you nor I can depart from our legal faculties, which are the maintenance of the constitution and the legal government without appearing to be traitors and disloyal to those from whom we derive our mission".[46] Juárez undoubtedly recognized the value of González Ortega's leadership and military ability at this crucial moment in the conflict and refrained from taking any action against him for fear of destroying the advantage which the Liberals possessed. Instead of receiving a reprimand from the Juárez government, therefore, González Ortega replaced Degollado as Commander-in-Chief of the Liberal forces.[47] Announcement of the appointment came on October 17, 1860.[48] González Ortega seems to have been in somewhat of a hurry to assume Degollado's position and to take charge of the funds which Degollado controlled. Degollado and others resisted until the official announcement of the change in command reached them.[49]

Justo Sierra has suggested that both González Ortega and Degollado were men of deep feeling, capable of rising to great heights in a crisis, but at the same time men who could not stand to see the people of Mexico bleeding for ideas they scarcely understood.[50] Certainly González Ortega was a man who often let sentiment interfere with practical politics. He was, however, as guilty of disloyalty to the government as Degollado.

Not long after receiving his promotion, González Ortega became ill with a fever. Leaving Zaragoza to carry on the siege of Guadalajara, he retired to San Juan del Teúl, Zacatecas, to recover his health. Although his illness was quite severe and there was even a rumor of his death, he rejoined his command in the last days of November.[51] In the meantime, Castillo sued for peace and turned Guadalajara over to Zaragoza's forces.[52] González Ortega was now free to march on Mexico City. Although there were still personal differences within the Liberal ranks, he managed to achieve a reasonable degree of unity with his army in preparation for the final assult on the capital.[53]

On December 9, 1860, the Liberals suffered a temporary setback at Toluca near Mexico City, where Miramón routed a large force under Berriozábal, Degollado, and Benito Gómez Farías, and took the Liberal leaders prisoner.[54] The enthusiasm of the Conservatives over this victory was shortlived, however, since the defeat, costly as it was to the Liberals, had not involved González Ortega's army. A few days later he appeared in the Valley of Mexico at the head of an army of 16,000 men from the brigades of Zacatecas, San Luis Potosí, Michoacán, Guanajuato, and Jalisco.

Miramón marched out from Mexico City with an army of about 8,000 men, and on the morning of December 22, attacked the Liberal army in the hills around San Miguel Calpulalpan. Within two hours the Liberals routed the badly outnumbered Conservative forces, and Miramón fled back into the city of Mexico.[55]

Miramón considered attempting to withstand a siege, but González Ortega's insistence on unconditional surrender dissuaded him.[56] On December 24, 1860, he abandoned the city, and the following day González Ortega entered it at the head of the first section of his victorious army.[57]The War of the Reform was over, but the Liberals would soon discover that the Conservatives were not completely defeated.

González Ortega immediately set about insuring law and order in the capital city. On December 27, he published a decree which condemned to death all persons accused of robbery and identified after being found with the stolen goods in their possession. On the following day the Reform Laws were published.[58] Juárez approved of these steps and advised González Ortega to work with Alatriste, the legal governor of the state of Mexico.[59]

To demonstrate the discipline of his troops and to add to the spectacle of the Liberal victory, González Ortega ordered his troops to the outskirts of the city to make a triumphal entry. On January 1, 1861, he rode into the capital at the head of 25,000 men. The people of the city gave him a hero's welcome, and he took full advantage of it. Catching sight of Degollado among the spectators, he halted the parade, calling him out and, handing him the flag, embraced and hailed him as the man who had made that day and that gesture possible. The crowd was greatly pleased by the act.[60]

González Ortega was the man of the hour, the man whose talent and fortune had given the Liberals their final triumph. Though he had been rather late in entering the conflict, he was now in the capital in command of thousands of troops and in an ideal position to place himself at the head of the government if he had any such desire. His rise had been rapid but he was definitely a man to be considered in Mexican national politics. He maintained his support of legality, however, and took only those steps which he believed necessary while awaiting the arrival of the constitutional president, Benito Juárez, from Veracruz.[61]

NOTES

1. Bancroft, *Mexico,* V, 776-781; Ralph Roeder, *Juárez and His Mexico* (New York, 1947, 2 vols.), I, 222.
2. Álvarez, *Estudios,* VI, 193.
3. Letters of M. Auza, August 6 and July 27, 1860, and numerous other letters written to González Ortega from Zacatecas in González Ortega Typescripts, I, II.
4. *Diario de Avisos,* March 17, 1860; Zamacois, *Historia de Méjico,* XV, 398; González Ortega, *Golpe,* p. 30.
5. González Ortega, *Golpe,* p. 30.
6. *Ibid.,* p. 31; Bancroft, *Mexico,* V, 781.

7. May 15, 1860.
8. *Diario de Avisos,* March 16, 1860, and other issues of the same paper in March, April and May.
9. *Ibid.,* May 22, 1860; Bancroft, *Mexico,* V, 783.
10. Rivera, *Anales,* p. 53; Cambre, *La guerra,* pp. 457-548. Ignacio Álvarez, writing about this battle, blamed the Conservative defeat on the stupidity of Ramírez in avoiding an earlier encounter with González Ortega. The result was that by the time of the battle the Conservative soldiers were completely exhausted. *Estudios,* VI, 195.
11. Sierra, *Juárez,* pp. 193-194.
12. Zamacois, *Historia de Mejico,* XIX, 415-416.
13. Juárez to González Ortega, Veracruz, July 6, 1860, and other letters in González Ortega Typescripts, I.
14. González Ortega, *Golpe,* p. 31; Vigil, *Reforma,* V, 424. See also Miguel Galindo y Galindo, *La gran década nacional, o relación histórica de la guerra de reforma, intervención extranjera y gobierno del Archiduque Maximiliano* (México, 1904-1906, 3 vols.), I, 422.
15. *Historia de Mejico,* XV, 423.
16. July 10, 1860.
17. *Diario de Avisos,* July 10, 1860; Zamacois, *Historia de Méjico,* XV, 425; and Planchet, *Cuestión,* p. 166, all tell substantially the same story.
18. *Diario de Avisos,* March 17, 1860.
19. Guillermo Prieto to Doblado, San Luis Potosí, June 26, 1860; Francisco Alatorre to Doblado, Zacatecas, July 9, 1860; and Doblado to Alatorre, Zacatecas, July 9, 1860, in Castañeda, "La guerra de reforma," pp. 189-192. Doblado denied any such purpose but the rumors were numerous.
20. González Ortega to Doblado, Zacatecas, April 29, 1860, in *ibid.,* pp. 183-184.
21. Just prior to the battle of Peñuelas, Degollado, as Commander in Chief of the Federal Army, had recognized an established fact by naming González Ortega military commander of Zacatecas, San Luis Potosí, Aguascalientes, and Durango. At the same time he refused an offer of appointment as a General of Brigade, saying that he preferred to remain a civilian volunteer. González Ortega, *Golpe,* pp. 30-31.
22. Cambre, *La guerra,* pp. 467-474; Bancroft, *Mexico,* V, 784. A report of the battle of Silao appears in the González Ortega Manuscripts (University of Texas), dated August 10, 1860.

23. Cited in Caldwell, "La Reforma," p. 204. See also *Apuntes,* pp. 41-43.
24. *Historia de Méjico,* XIX, 415-416.
25. Degollado to González Ortega, San Juan de Llanos, August 11, 1860, and other letters in González Ortega Typescripts, II. The military appointment was announced in the general order of August 12, and in a letter to González Ortega, August 17, 1860, in *ibid.*
26. *Diario de Avisos,* August 16, 1860.
27. Zamacois, *Historia de Méjico,* XV, 467-469; Caldwell, "La Reforma," p. 203.
28. *Diario de Avisos,* August 21 and 22, 1860.
29. González Ortega to Foreign Ministers and Charge d'affairs in Mexico, Querétaro, August 20, 1860, in González Ortega Typescripts, II; Degollado to González Ortega, Guanajuato, August 22, 1860, in González Ortega Manuscripts. See also Álvarez, *Estudios,* VI, 197.
30. Pacheco to González Ortega, México, August 24 and September 4, 1860, and González Ortega to Pacheco, Querétaro, August 31, 1860, in *Diario de Avisos,* September 10, 1860. The first letter from Pacheco and other replies from foreign representatives will be found in González Ortega Typescripts, II.
31. *Apuntes,* p. 43; Bancroft, *Mexico,* V, 787; Roeder, *Juárez,* I, 245.
32. González Ortega to Nicasio Trevino, September 18, 1860, in *Diario de Avisos,* October 9, 1860.
33. Berriozábal to González Ortega, Celaya, August 26, 1860, in González Ortega Typescripts, II.
34. August 28, 1860.
35. González Ortega to Morales, August 31, 1860, in *Diario de Avisos,* October 25, 1860.
36. Degollado to González Ortega, Guanajuato, August 29, 1860, in Genero García (ed.), "Don Santos Degollado, sus manifiestos, campanas, destitución militar, enjuiciamiento, rehabilitación, muerte, funerales y honores póstumos," in *Documentos Inéditos o muy raros* (México, 1906-1913, 36 vols.), XI, 114-116.
37. Doblado to Degollado, Guanajuato, September 10, 1860; Doblado to Echagaray, Guanajuato, September 4, 1860; and manifesto of Degollado, September 12, 1860, in *ibid.,* 124-127, 122, 117-121. See also Castañeda, "La guerra de reforma, " p. 243, and Emparán to Mathew, September 16, 1860, in *British and Foreign State Papers* (London, 1868), LI, 557.
38. Degollado to Mathew, Lagos, September 21, 1860, in García (ed.), "Don Santos Degollado," pp. 130-133; *Diario de Avisos,* Novem-

ber 11, 1860. Roeder, *Juárez,* I, 248-255, discounts the initial influence on Degollado by Mathew. The entire affair was motivated, Roeder believes, by the psychological breakdown of Degollado when he realized the possible consequences of the seizure of the *conducta.* At the same time there was clearly the possibility that Doblado and González Ortega had encouraged him hoping to see him discredited, because there had been a growing dislike of Degollado in Liberal ranks. See also Bancroft, *Mexico,* V, 788, and González Ortega, *Golpe,* p. 43.

39. Degollado to Juárez, Lagos, September 23 and 24, 1860, in Archivo Juárez Manuscripts, Biblioteca Nacional, Mexico City. The author is indebted to Professor Walter V. Scholes for the use of his notes on this collection.

40. Unsigned letter of September 31, 1860, in González Ortega Typescripts, II; González Ortega to Degollado, Belem, September 30, 1860, in García (ed.), "Don Santos Degollado," pp. 141-142; and Degollado to González Ortega, Lagos, October 12, 1860, in Degollado Manuscripts.

41. Juárez to Degollado, Veracruz, October 4, 1860, in Archivo Juárez Manuscripts; Juárez to González Ortega, Veracruz, October 10, 1860, in González Ortega Typescripts, II.

42. González Ortega to Treviño, Lagos, September 18, 1860, in *Diario de Avisos,* October 9, 1860.

43. González Ortega to Castillo, San Pedro, September 22 and 23; Castillo to González Ortega, Guadalajara, September 23, 1860, in Cambre, *La guerra,* pp. 542-544. See also *Diario de Avisos,* October 8, 1860.

44. González Ortega to Degollado, San Pedro, September 26, 1860, in González Ortega Typescripts, II.

45. *La Bandera Roja,* no date, cited in Cambre, *La guerra,* pp. 569-573; Luis Verdia Pérez, *Historia particular del estado de Jalisco* (Guadalajara, 1911, 3 vols.), III, 112-113; Bulnes, *Juárez y las revoluciones,* p. 579; González Ortega, *Golpe,* p. 46. González Ortega himself certainly did not place his actions in the same category with those of Degollado and in fact assured Degollado that his was the only voice of disapproval. González Ortega to Degollado, Belem, October 2, 1860, in González Ortega, Typescripts, II.

46. Cited in Roeder, *Juárez,* I, 257. See also Degollado to Doblado, Lagos, September 30, 1860, in González Ortega Typescripts, II.

47. Perhaps González Ortega's explanation of his actions and his rejection of Degollado's plan were partially satisfactory to Juárez. González Ortega to Juárez, San Pedro, October 6, 1860, in González

Ortega Manuscripts.
48. Ignacio de la Llave to Degollado, Veracruz, October 10, 1860, in Documentos relativos de la reforma (University of Texas); Llave to González Ortega, Veracruz, October 10, 1860, in García (ed.), "Don Santos Degollado," pp. 149-150; D y L, *Legislación,* VIII, 754-755; *Archivo Mexicano,* IV, 377-380.
49. Degollado to Doblado and Ignacio Ramírez to Doblado, Tepatitlán, October 10, 1860, in Castaneda (ed.), "La guerra de reforma," pp. 224-226.
50. Sierra, *Juárez,* p. 202.
51. Prieto to González Ortega, Guanajuato, November 20, 1860; Degollado to González Ortega, Tepatitlán, October 16, 1860; and Doblado to González Ortega, Guanajuato, November 16, 1860, in González Ortega Typescripts, II; *Diario de Avisos,* November 22, 1860.
52. *Diario de Avisos,* November 15, 1860; Álvarez, *Estudios,* VI, 200.
53. Various letters of November and December, 1860, in González Ortega Typescripts, III; Bancroft, *Mexico,* V, 792.
54. Rivera, *Anales,* p. 57.
55. Vigil, *Reforma,* p. 443; *Apuntes,* pp. 47-50; Official report of González Ortega to the Minister of War cited in González Ortega, *Golpe,* p. 47.
56. González Ortega to Doblado, Tepeji del Río, December 24, 1860, in Castañeda (ed.), "La guerra de reforma," pp. 265-266; Bancroft, *Mexico,* V, 794.
57. Zamacois, *Historia de Méjico,* XV, 521; Rivera, *Anales,* p. 58.
58. Porfirio Díaz, *Memorias, 1830-1867* (México, 1922, 2 vols.), I, 212; Rivera, *Anales,* p. 58. The rather large number of letters in the González Ortega Manuscripts testify to the amount of official business transacted by González Ortega before Juárez arrived in the capital.
59. Juárez to González Ortega, December 29, 1860, in González Ortega, *Golpe,* p. 49.
60. Degollado's diary in García (ed.), "Don Santos Degollado," p. 233; Prieto to Doblado, Mexico, January 2, 1861, in Castañeda (ed.), "La guerra de reforma," p. 269; *El Monitor Republicano,* January 1, 1861, cited in Pérez Verdia, *Jalisco,* pp. 125-126.
61. González Ortega to Doblado, Palacio Nacional de México, December 28, 1860, in Castañeda (ed.), "La guerra de reforma," p. 268; González Ortega, *Golpe,* p. 53.

IV
Rivalry with Juárez

On the morning of January 11, 1861, Juárez arrived in the capital and by evening of the same day had announced a policy of moderation and held his first cabinet meeting. The formation of a complete cabinet was one of the first problems which had to be met, since during the war some of the ministerial posts had not been filled and some men occupied several portfolios. González Ortega was offered the post of Secretary of War, which he accepted on January 13.[1] Other members of the cabinet were Juan Antonio de la Fuente as Secretary of Justice, Melchor Ocampo as Minister of Foreign Relations and interim Treasurer, José Emparán as *Fomento,* and Ignacio de la Llave as *Gobernación.*[2]

It became apparent immediately that the policy of moderation Juárez had adopted toward the defeated enemy was not going to satisfy public opinion, which demanded some form of retaliation after three years of violent conflict. The ringleaders of the reaction had escaped after the battle of Calpulalpam, Márquez and Zuloaga into the interior and Miramón to Cuba. Miramón's brother-in-law and principal Conservative minister, Isidoro Díaz, was captured, however, and on him fell the full fury of public opinion. After ordering his execution, Juárez commuted the sentence to banishment and, at the same time, decreed a policy of amnesty.[3]

Francisco Zarco, editor of the most powerful paper of the Liberal party, *El Siglo Diez y Nueve,* raised the alarm. As soon as the rumor of Díaz' pardon and the general amnesty appeared, Zarco wrote: "If this happens, farewell freedom, farewell justice, farewell all public order!...It is true that justice can be administered with mercy, and that our Constitution gives the Executive the right to pardon; but that pardon must not be a scandal or a crime against society as a whole."[4] The cry was taken up by the remainder of the press, the political clubs, and the public in general. Zarco continued to attack Juárez. He granted that, in the absence of a congress, the executive had to act independently in many cases, but he believed that Juárez was overstepping the bounds of necessity. Zarco was primarily concerned with the separation of judicial and executive powers. He felt that the time had come for the judicial branch of the government to begin operating, and that the question of amnesty should be decided by that branch.[5]

This dispute reached a climax on January 17 when Juárez ordered the expulsion of Lazaro de la Garza y Ballesteros, the Archbishop of Mexico, and Bishops Clemente de Jesús Munguia, Joaquín Madrid, Pedro Espinosa, and Pedro Barajas.[6]This action was denounced by Zarco as a violation of the Constitution of 1857. Fuente resigned from the government as a direct result of the order.[7]This act by Juárez was seen as another invasion of the rights of the judiciary, and the major portion of the press continued to attack the government. It was not necessarily the desire for stronger punishment of the bishops that caused the attack but rather the belief that Juárez should have allowed the judiciary to make the decision. The pressure of public opinion was not lost on the other members of the cabinet, and on the afternoon of January 17, Ocampo, Llave, González Ortega, and Emparán submitted their resignations.[8]Evidently González Ortega's resignation was not accepted.

Ignacio Ramírez was called upon to aid in the formation of a new cabinet, but discussions took place for three days before the actual announcement of its members could be made. Zarco pointed out that the delay resulted from the lack of unity of thought. He felt, however, that the new cabinet should see quite clearly what public opinion demanded, for never before had there been such unanimity of public expression.[9]The new cabinet, as announced on January 21, consisted of Guillermo Prieto, Treasury; González Ortega, War; Zarco, Foreign Relations; Pedro Ogazón, *Gobernación;* Ramírez, Justice; and Miguel Auza, *Fomento.* Apparently this cabinet was appointed with a view toward including some of the most popular figures of the time.[10]

While this ministerial crisis was going on, the country was in the midst of a presidential election by virtue of a decree issued at Veracruz on November 6, 1860, when a Liberal victory had seemed certain.[11]The leading candidates for the presidency were Juárez, González Ortega, and Miguel Lerdo de Tejada. González Ortega was supported by a large part of the army and a good portion of the revolutionary clubs which were organized all over Mexico to support a particular candidate. He could also depend upon support from many of the newspapers in Mexico.[12]In addition, the Liberal leader of Guanajuato, Doblado, whose influence was considerable, had voiced his support of González Ortega as early as January, 1861.[13]

Undoubtedly González Ortega felt that his chances of election were extremely good. On March 14, in fact, he accepted the honorary presidency of the Club Reformista, a revolutionary society which had been extremely critical of Juárez and his administration.[14]He also received numerous communications from individuals who supported his candidacy.[15]

Lerdo's death of typhus fever on March 22, after the elections had been held but before the results were known, left a large part of the opposition to Juárez without a leader. It was only natural that many of these men should rally around González Ortega as a man who was powerful enough to defeat Juárez. Certainly González Ortega, like Lerdo, had developed the habit of running his department independently and of ignoring the president, politely or impolitely.[16]

Pressure upon Juárez, which had subsided somewhat after the January crisis, began to increase. Newspaper criticism mounted, and political clubs attempted to discredit the administration. In the latter part of March the Club Reformista even sent a note to Juárez demanding that the entire cabinet be removed and replaced by men who conformed more nearly to the desires and aspirations of club members. Juárez ignored this demand as well as the attacks.[17]

Meanwhile the financial plight of the government provided additional grounds for criticism by the opposition. The combination of old and new debts, added to the bad management and corruption which had been inflicted on the country in the past, made the straightening out of Mexican finances almost impossible. The onus of this task fell primarily upon Prieto, but the entire administration came in for its share of blame. Finally, on April 6, 1861, Prieto admitted his inability to arrange the finances satisfactorily and resigned from the government.[18] Faced with growing unpopularity because of his continued association with the government, González Ortega demanded that Juárez dismiss Zarco and Ramírez from the cabinet because of their disrepute. When this demand was refused, González Ortega resigned from the ministry.[19]

In his resignation González Ortega stated that it was clear to him from the attitude of the press and various political circulars that public opinion was against the cabinet. Since the president had rejected his proposal he felt that he should remove himself from the ministry. The letter ended with protestations of his respect for legality and the assertion that he would remain at the head of the Division of Zacatecas to sustain democratic institutions. Juárez accepted this resignation on the same day. In answering it for the government, Zarco stated that González Ortega had confused public opinion with the noise of a club which possessed no significance, and that he had been moved to act by a minority which had no real political principles. In conclusion Zarco informed González Ortega that he should await action by the national government on the question of command of the Division of Zacatecas.[20]

González Ortega answered Zarco with a blistering attack on the administration. Public opinion was against the cabinet, he said, for a variety of reasons. The government had enacted a large number of laws and decrees without careful thought and with too much favoritism. The government had failed to restore peace to Mexico even in victory, and the people identified with the revolution were not sufficiently represented. As for the question of his right to command the Division of Zacatecas, he replied that the force in question was made up entirely of the national guard of the state, which was under his exclusive control as governor. He intended to remain at the head of the division, and he questioned whether the desire for his removal was not merely to satisfy the personal interests of the government.[21]

After another exchange of letters in which Juárez maintained his constitutional right to exercise authority over the national guard, Juárez notified González Ortega that he had been appointed to command the Division of Zacatecas. Juárez hoped that González Ortega's valuable service would not be lost to the nation now that he had resigned from the cabinet.[22]

For a few days the split between Juárez and González Ortega caused a great deal of excitement throughout the country. The press commented extensively on it and a public demonstration took place in front of the National Palace. Almost without exception, however, the press rallied to the president's defense. Although the disturbance was purely ministerial, there was the constant fear that something more drastic would result. Manuel Zamacona, who had replaced Zarco as editor of *El Siglo Diez y Nueve,* asked what had happened to the hero of Capulalpam. He expressed disbelief that this was the same man the country had honored, and he felt certain that some evil influences had been brought to bear on González Ortega. He concluded by urging González Ortega to return to the government and the party which he had deserted.[23]

One of the political clubs sent a commission of its members to urge Juárez not to accept González Ortega's resignation, but Juárez refused to see them after learning the purpose of their visit. Zacatecas was ready to pronounce against the president, but no actual violence took place. This conflict did not result in revolution, as many feared it would because of the firmness of Juárez and González Ortega's refusal to lend his support to violence.[24]

Calm was restored on May 1 when González Ortega issued a manifesto to the Mexican people denying that he had sanctioned a revolutionary movement, either by some overt act or by implication. He cautioned the people that the war was now over and the time had come to use the pen and not the sword. He voiced his intention to support the legal government and to do all in his power to reduce the danger of civil war. He concluded by calling upon the Mexican people to have faith in their public men now the hour of battle was past.[25]The Mexican people, meanwhile, were becoming more and more alarmed over the large-scale guerrilla warfare which was going on throughout Mexico. As previously stated, the end of the War of the Reform did not mean the end of the Conservative opposition to the Liberal government. In various parts of the country large bands of former Conservative soldiers continued to attack towns and villages and generally make the roads and highways unsafe. These bands were led by former Conservative officers, of whom the most outstanding were Márquez, Mejía, and Zuloaga. Most of the opposition to these guerrillas had been supplied by the various state governors, while the federal government had so far been unable to send out a force which could win a decisive victory over the major reactionary leaders.

At the beginning of June the nation became even more aroused when Ocampo, who had retired to his ranch in Michoacán, was seized by one of the guerrilla bands, taken to the camp of Márquez and Zuloaga, and executed.[26]Santos Degollado requested and received the permission of the government to lead an army against the Conservatives. On June 15, 1861, however, Degollado was surprised at Salazar, between Mexico City and Toluca, and killed in the battle which followed.[27]

On June 4, González Ortega volunteered his services to the government against the Conservative forces, although he had already made plans to return to Zacatecas. On June 8 he was commissioned to raise forces, and within three days he departed from Mexico City.[28]He pursued Márquez until June 25, when he returned to the capital without having made contact with the enemy. Departing again on July 2, González Ortega pursued Márquez and his army for the next six weeks while attempting to corner him and force him to fight. Throughout this time González Ortega sent numerous requests to Mexico City for funds and supplies, which were evidently not furnished in sufficient quantities. At the same time, some officials criticized González Ortega for demanding more supplies than were necessary.[29]His supporters in the capital informed him that Juárez expected Márquez to defeat him, thus removing him from the political scene. They maintained that this plot made it imperative for him to make his bid for the presidency. There is no indication, however, that González Ortega seriously considered the suggestion, although some such act to restore Comonfort to the presidency was rumored.[30]Early in August González Ortega located Márquez, Zuloaga, and several other Conservative leaders with about 2,500 men at Jalatlaco. Porfirio Díaz, who was serving under González Ortega's command attacked the enemy without orders. When the remainder of González Ortega's command joined him he defeated and dispersed the reactionary forces.[31]This news was received in Mexico City with salvos of artillery and public demonstrations, showing the importance that the people of Mexico attached to the triumph, even though it represented temporary relief and not the complete defeat of the Conservative forces.[32]

While González Ortega had been preparing to leave Mexico City in June, the national congress constituted itself as an electoral college to count the votes in the presidential election. After some delay and much argument Juárez was declared elected on June 11, 1861, with a total of 5,289 votes against 1,989 votes for Lerdo and 1,846 for González Ortega.[33]A group of deputies opposed to Juárez immediately proposed that the congress constitute itself as a national convention and create a Committee of Public Safety to administer the government. Under this plan a triumvirate composed of González Ortega, Doblado, and Uraga would have made up the committee with Juárez, Ogazón, and Degollado as alternates.[34]When Juárez opposed this plan there was talk of forcing him to concede the presidency to Gonzalez Ortega. During all of these proceedings González Ortega was in the field with an army, and there is no evidence that he participated in such movements or even condoned them.[35]

The anti-Juárez faction, with or without González Ortega's approval, still had plans for his succession to the presidency. On June 27, 1861, Congress named González Ortega as interim president of the Supreme Court. Constitutionally the power of election was vested in the people rather than in Congress, but very little opposition was raised since the Congress evidently felt that some provision should be made in the event of an emergency.[36]In connection with his selection to the head of the Supreme Court, González Ortega wrote to his wife on July 1, telling her that Juárez had done everything in his power to prevent the election because he was tottering in the presidential chair and was afraid of falling once González Ortega ascended to the Supreme Court. He continued, "I have offered no opposition to him although I despise his government which is entirely discredited."[37]

Upon his return to Mexico City following the battle of Jalatlaco, González Ortega's first official act was to appear before the permanent deputation of congress to take over the post as president of the court. Since the military victory and the new political post had increased his reputation, the speech he made on this occasion attracted considerable attention. It was only natural that many persons detected hostility to the government in his statements in view of the rather continuous moves that had been made to eliminate Juárez and place himself in the presidency.[38]In this discourse he protested his own lack of training for the position on the court, and he assured his audience that if he ever became an obstacle to the government and the progress of reform he would resign. The point which aroused special comment in the press was his warning against the possibility of military victories without practical results. He intimated that the government was too concerned with punishing a few reactionaries and was not trying to establish peace for the people of Mexico so that the reform principles could be implanted.[39]

Much of the press--even some of the papers that opposed González Ortega--argued that there was no hidden meaning in his speech, and that he was only expressing a sincere belief in the need for liberal unity. Some also pointed out that the speech was vague and full of generalities, making it impossible to build an opposition program around it.[40]It would appear that those who wished to read opposition into the speech continued to do so, however, and anti-Juárez activities still revolved around González Ortega's name.

On August 30 an extraordinary session of congress was opened, and on September 7 a petition signed by fifty-one deputies was addressed to Juárez requesting that he resign as president in view of his failure to advance the reform program and his personal disrepute in the eyes of the people. While González Ortega's name was not mentioned in the petition, it was generally understood that should Juárez resign, González Ortega would become acting president.[41]On the same day another petition voicing confidence in the administration was signed by fifty-two members of congress. It expressed the belief that, even though Juárez had made errors, his removal from office was not the answer to the problem. Public statements immediately began to appear in support of one or the other of the two petitions, though there is no indication that Juárez ever considered stepping down.[42]

Another event, even more indicative of the state of relations between González Ortega and Juárez, took place at about the same time that the congressional petitions appeared. The victory of Jalatlaco, though important, had not ended the struggle against the reactionary forces in Mexico, and it soon became necessary for the government to undertake new operations against Conservative groups. On August 23, therefore, González Ortega was ordered to take the divisions of Zacatecas, Guanajuato, and

Querétaro, and continue the campaign against Mejía and other Conservative leaders operating in the mountains north of Mexico City.

González Ortega accepted the command and requested permission from congress to absent himself from the Supreme Court for this purpose.[43]After some debate, Congress granted him permission. During the next few days he argued with Minister of War Zaragoza concerning the money and resources needed to conduct the campaign. On September 9, after his requests had not been met, he advised the government that under the circumstances he could not accept the command and be responsible for the outcome of the campaign.[44]On the following day congress accepted his resignation with the comment that even if his requests had not been met, the government had provided him with sufficient resources to carry out his mission.[45]

On September 12, 1861, Doblado was named commander-in-chief of the Liberal forces and instructed to carry out the campaign.[46]At the same time Juárez ordered González Ortega to turn command of the forces of Zacatecas over to General Francisco Alatorre. González Ortega protested this order on the grounds that he had not resigned his command of the state troops and that, as constitutional governor of Zacatecas, he had the right and the duty to continue at the head of said forces.[47]At the same time, he wrote to Doblado expressing his confusion over the government's orders and requesting Doblado to come to his aid. Doblado advised him that he could do nothing more than follow the orders of the government.[48]González Ortega meanwhile had moved his forces to Querétaro, where he received orders from Juárez to proceed to Zacatecas and turn the command over to Alatorre.[49]

The situation evidently remained critical until Doblado intervened and placated Juárez, because on October 2, 1861, he named González Ortega second-in-command of the army under Doblado.[50]This dissipated the fears that González Ortega was holding onto an army in order to establish himself at the head of the government. As F. de P. Serrano wrote in *El Siglo Diez y Nueve,* Mexico had become so accustomed to the personal ambitions and revolutions of its *caudillos* that some move by González Ortega was honestly anticipated, but his conduct had done much to remove this fear.[51]González Ortega's defense of legality had been demonstrated once more, but the fear that he would act illegally would plague him throughout his public career.

In the midst of these domestic problems the Mexican government suddenly found itself faced with the far more serious problem of foreign intervention. Mexico was still to be denied the privilege of peacefully working out her political problems.

NOTES

1. Ocampo to González Ortega, Mexico, January 12, 1861, and González Ortega to Ocampo, México, January 13, 1861, in *Archivo Mexicano,* V, 30, 47-48. The appointment was officially announced on January 16, 1861 (*Ibid.,* 59.). González Ortega was temporarily considered by Juárez for the post of Secretary of the Treasury, but González Ortega preferred the military office. *Archivos privados de D. Benito Juárez y D. Pedro Santacilia* (México, 1928), p. 279.
2. *El Siglo XIX,* January 15, 1861. The posts of *Fomento* and *Gobernación* have no exact English equivalent and consequently will be given their Spanish names throughout this study. The post of *Gobernación* was created to relieve the Minister of Justice from interior administration not closely connected with justice and ecclesiastical affairs. The department of *Fomento* embraced public works, trade, colonization and related matters. Both of these departments have duties found in the Department of the Interior in the United States with other additional duties.
3. *Ibid.,* January 16, 1861; Roeder, *Juárez,* I, 271.
4. January 16, 1861.
5. *El Siglo XIX,* January 17, 1861.
6. D y L, *Legislación,* IX, 12.
7. *El Siglo XIX,* January 17, 1861; Rafael de Zayas Enríquez, *Benito Juárez, su vida — su obra* (México, 1906), p. 114.
8. *El Siglo XIX,* January 18 and 19, 1861; *Archivo Mexicano,* V, 74-75. Ramírez to Doblado with postscript by Prieto, México, Janu-

ary 16, 1861, in Doblado Typescripts, relates the loss of popularity by González Ortega due to his association with the government.
9. *El Siglo XIX,* January 18 and 19, 1861.
10. *Ibid,* January 21, 1861. Though it is impossible to determine how much influence he had, prior to his resignation, González Ortega, had suggested the inclusion of Ogazón, the governor of Jalisco, and Miguel Auza, the acting governor of Zacatecas, in a new cabinet. González Ortega to Doblado, Mexico, January 17, 1861, in Doblado Typescripts ; and Ogazón to González Ortega, Tepic, January 29, 1861, in González Ortega Typescripts, IV. Auza was serving as acting governor of Zacatecas as a result of a decree by the state legislature of January 16, which declared González Ortega interim governor. Notice of this action by M. Auza, Zacatecas, January 16, 1861, in González Ortega Typescripts, IV. See also *El Siglo XIX,* January 27, 1861, and *El Pajaro Verde,* January 22, 1861.
11. D Y L, *Legislación,* VIII, 760.
12. Roeder, *Juárez,* I, 295; Zayas Enríquez, *Juárez,* p. 116. *El Siglo XIX,* January 17, 1861, states that a new paper, *El Porvenir,* was to be founded to support González Ortega. *El Boletín de Noticias,* January 25 and 27, 1861, refers to a Club González Ortega in México City.
13. Doblado to González Ortega, Guanajuato, January 4, 1861, in González Ortega Typescripts, I; González Ortega to Doblado, México, February 6, 1861, in Doblado Typescripts. The Doblado letter is incorrectly dated 1860, but this would not be unusual so soon after the beginning of a new year.
14. *El Siglo XIX,* March 14, 1861.
15. One such letter was a rather amusing one from former subscribers to *El Pobre Diablo* enclosing two copies of that paper to remind González Ortega of his former promises. Jesús M. Castañeda, Carlos Fernández, Rafael Díaz to González Ortega, Calchiuetes, February 20, 1861, in González Ortega Typescripts, IV. It is not surprising that González Ortega received an almost unanimous vote in Zacatecas for the presidency. Juan F. Román to González Ortega, Zacatecas, February 8, 1861, in *ibid.,* II; and Severo Cosio to González Ortega, Zacatecas, February 18, 1861, in González Ortega Manuscripts.
16. Guillermo Prieto, *Leciones de historia patria* (México, 1893), p. 411; Roeder, *Juárez,* I, p. 295.
17. *El Siglo XIX,* April 8, 1861; Galindo y Galindo, *Gran década,* II, 35; Vigil, *Reforma,* p. 457.
18. *El Siglo XIX,* April 6, 1861.

19. González Ortega to Secretary of Relations, México, April 6,1861, in González Ortega Typescripts, IV; *El Siglo XIX,* April 7, 1861.
20. Zarco to González Ortega, México, April 6, 1861, in González Ortega Typescripts, IV. The club referred to was probably the Club Reformista which congratulated González Ortega on his resignation. Miguel García Munive to González Ortega, April 7, 1861, and reply, April 10, 1861, in González Ortega Manuscripts. The action was backed by other political clubs, however. Sociedad de Socorros Mutuos to Honorary President González Ortega, April 9, 1861, and Antonio P. Mata, president of Club Rojo de Guerrero in Morelia, to González Ortega, April 17, 1861, and reply, May 10, 1861, in *ibid.*
21. González Ortega to Zarco, México, April 7, 1861, in González Ortega Typescripts, IV. González Ortega had been officially elected governor on April 3. President of Supreme Tribunal to González Ortega, Zacatecas, April 3, 1861, and letter of reply, México, April 17, 1861, in González Ortega Manuscripts.
22. González Ortega to Zarco, Mexico, April 9, 1861, in González Ortega Typescripts, IV; Gonzalez Ortega, *Golpe,* pp. 58-60.
23. *El Siglo XIX,* April 9, 1861.
24. González Ortega to Doblado, México, April 8, 1861, and Antonio Aguado to Doblado, México, April 8, 1861, in Doblado Typescripts. See alsoVigil, *Reforma,* p. 457, and Zayas Enríquez, *Juárez,* p. 117.
25. González Ortega to the Nation, México, May 1, 1861, in González Ortega Typescripts, IV. See also unsigned letter to Doblado, April 16, 1861, in Doblado Typescripts. This manifesto did not stop the hope by some that González Ortega might still be elected president. Carlos Butterfield wrote to González Ortega from New York on May 6, 1861, expressing the hope that he would be elected and asking to represent him in the United States. González Ortega Manuscripts. The British Ambassador to México, George B. Mathew, still felt that González Ortega would be elected. Mathew to Lord J. Russell, May 12, 1861, in *British and Foreign State Papers,* LII, 250-254.
26. Vigil, *Reforma,* pp. 454-456, 460.
27. Rivera, *Anales,* p. 67.
28. *El Siglo XIX,* June 8 and 10, 1861. See also Galindo y Galindo, *Gran década,* II, 64.
29. González Ortega to Minister of War, Cuernavaca, July 17, 1861, in González Ortega Typescripts, V. See also Zamacois, *Historia de Méjico,* XV, 723, and Vigil, *Reforma,* pp. 463-467.

30. Unsigned letter to González Ortega, México, July 23, 1861, and M. Cabezut to González Ortega, México, July 25, 1861, in González Ortega Manuscripts.

31. González Ortega to Manuel Alas, Governor of Mexico, Jalatlaco, August 14, 1861, in González Ortega Typescripts, V; *El Siglo XIX,* August 15, 1861. An official report of the action at Jalatlaco by González Ortega appears in *Archivo del General Porfirio Díaz* (México, 1947, 2 vols.), I, 265-269. Díaz in his *Memorias,* I, 219-226, alleges that González Ortega, who had presidential ambitions, was annoyed at the success of the Oaxaca troops, which were loyal to Juárez, and failed to give them credit for the victory. It should be pointed out that González Ortega not only commended the Oaxaca troops for their bravery, but also recommended Díaz for a promotion, which he received. See Zaragoza to González Ortega, México, August 26, 1866, in González Ortega Typescripts, V, for the promotion. Díaz did recall this in a conversation with González Ortega's grandson in 1910. González Ortega, *Golpe,* p. 69.

32. *El Siglo XIX,* August, 20, 1861. An alleged attempt to assassinate the French minister was made during one of the celebrations, but an investigation revealed nothing to substantiate the charges. *U. S. House Executive Documents,* 37 Cong., 2 Sess. (1861-1862), No. 100, 122-133.

33. Vigil, *Reforma,* p. 469. A total of 512 votes were cast for other candidates.

34. Juan Ortiz Careaga to Doblado, México, June 12, 1861, in Doblado Typescripts; Zayas Enríquez, *Juárez,* p. 117.

35. *El Siglo XIX,* June 18 and 28, 1861.

36. *Ibid.,* June 27, 1861; Zamacois, *Historia de Méjico,* XV, 719. Both the American and British representatives in Mexico reported that not only was every possible peaceful step being taken to force Juárez out, but that the attempt would probably succeed. Thomas Corwin to Secretary Seward, June 29, 1861, in *U.S. House Executive Documents,* 37 Cong., 1861, 2 Sess., No. 100, 12; Sir Charles L. Wyke to Lord J. Russell, June 28, in *British and Foreign State Papers,* LII, 283-285.

37. July 1, 1861, in González Ortega, *Golpe,* pp. 64-65. This writer has been unable to discover much information about González Ortega's wife other than the name, Mercedes Mercado de Ortega on her letter to him from Teúl dated June 20, 1858, in González Ortega Typescripts, I. The marriage probably took place some time prior to the Revolution of Ayutla when González Ortega was living in Zacatecas, and the couple was separated a great deal of the time.

38. Vigil, *Reforma,* p. 469.
39. Speech by González Ortega on taking possession of the presidency of the Supreme Court, August 20, 1861, in González Ortega Typescripts, II; *El Siglo XIX,* August 22, 1861.
40. *El Siglo XIX,* August 23 and 29, 1861; *El Constitucional* cited in *ibid.,* August 28, 1861. See also Vigil, *Reforma,* p. 469.
41. *El Siglo XIX,* September 7, 1861; Zamacois, *Historia de Méjico,* XV, 749.
42. Buenrostro, *Historia del congresos,* III, contains a number of such letters. Letter to Manuel M. O. de Montellano signed by 28 citizens backing the request for resignation, 456; letter of September 15, 1861, to state governors urging them to speak up and answering an earlier letter to the governors by Juárez, 469-471; letters denouncing González Ortega by Eugenio Quesada, September 8, 1861, and by Germán de Uslar, no date, 453-456, 493-499.
43. González Ortega to Secretary of Congress, México, August 30, 1861, in González Ortega Typescripts, V.
44. Juárez, *Archivos privados,* pp. 304-305; *El Siglo XIX,* September 5, 1861. See also Juárez to Doblado, August 29, 1861, in Doblado Typescripts.
45. *El Siglo XIX,* September 12, 1861; José Velázquez to Doblado, September 11, 1861, in Doblado Typescripts.
46. Juárez to Doblado, México, September 13, 1861; Zaragoza to Doblado, México, September 13, 1861, in *ibid.*
47. González Ortega to Zaragoza, Arroyo Zarco, September 21, 1861, in *ibid.* It should be remembered that González Ortega was named governor of Zacatecas in January and, in spite of his election to the presidency of the court, was still recognized as such in his state.
48. Two letters from González Ortega to Doblado, La Soledad, September 23, 1861, in Doblado Typescripts.
49. Juárez to Doblado, México, September 28, 1861, in *ibid.*
50. Doblado to González Ortega, San Luis Potosi, September 29, 1861, in Archivo Juárez Manuscripts; González Ortega to Zaragoza, Queretaro, September 29, 1861, in González Ortega Typescripts, V; *El Siglo XIX,* October 2, 1861.
51. October 4, 1861.

V
"Defender of Puebla"

At the close of the War of the Reform the Juárez government faced a series of complicated problems in its relations with Britain, France, and Spain. The primary problem was financial. Not only did Mexico owe outstanding debts to these European nations, but during the fighting Mexicans had done damage to the property of their nationals, for which claims had been filed. While Juárez was willing to assume responsibility for those claims which could be proved genuine, there was not enough money in the treasury to meet domestic expenses which had to be satisfied before the foreign obligations. There were only threats of foreign action, however, until July 17, 1861, when Juárez issued a decree suspending payment on the foreign debts of Mexico for a period of two years.[1]

The Spanish and French representatives recommended immediate armed intervention, but the British Minister, Sir Charles Wyke, urged a more moderate policy and suggested that the occupation of some of the harbors of Mexico would produce the desired effect. Spain favored a more aggressive policy, partly because of a long-standing desire to regain some kind of control over her erstwhile colony and partly because of a desire to collect the debts. In France, too, important forces were moving that country toward intervention with or without any financial excuse. A group of Mexican refugees had been attempting for some time to spread the gospel of monarchy for Mexico. Its outstanding members were José Manuel Hidalgo y Esnaurrizar, a young diplomat; J. M. Gutiérrez de Estrada, a long-time monarchist; and General Juan N. Almonte, minister to France in the Miramón government and illegitimate son of the revolutionary leader José María Morelos. The efforts of this group, coupled with the advice of the Count de Saligny, French Minister to Mexico, made Napoleon III receptive to the Spanish suggestion for intervention, while the British government entered into the project to protect her own interests. The result was the Treaty of London, October 31, 1861, which provided for consultation among the three powers with the object of organizing an expedition to occupy Mexican ports in an effort to collect the debts owed by Mexico. There was no announced intention of interfering with the right of the Mexican people to select their own government.[2]

When news of the threatened intervention reached Mexico, Juárez issued orders to strengthen Veracruz and other points along the coast. At the same time he began negotiations with Britain, Mexico's chief creditor, in hope of forestalling actual intervention. The British Minister drove a hard bargain, but in November, 1861, he and Minister of Foreign Relations Manuel M. Zamacona reached an agreement[3]which settled every question at stake between the two countries. Unfortunately, this agreement was not approved by the Mexican congress because of the provision for British intervention in the collection of custom duties in Mexico.[4]

Arguments over this proposed Zamacona-Wyke agreement brought about a ministerial crisis early in December. Zamacona resigned and Juárez named Doblado to the post of Minister of Foreign Relations and president of the cabinet[5]Doblado immediately asked the congress to grant the executive extraordinary powers to insure the preservation of national independence and the reform laws. On December 11, four days before adjournment, congress granted the request.

With the failure of the Zamacona-Wyke agreement, the British agreed to the occupation of Mexican ports, and on December 14, 1861, a Spanish contingent of 6,000 men arrived at Veracruz. On January 9, 1862, A French squadron landed 2,000 marines and 600 zouaves and soldiers of the line. The English sent only 800 marines, an indication of their reluctance to join in the project. During the next few months discussions between the invaders and representatives of the Juárez government revealed that the French planned to impose impossible conditions on the

Mexican government. Disgusted with Napoleon's scheming, Spaniards and British decided to leave Mexico. In April the Spanish and British representatives notified Juárez of their governments' decision to withdraw and added that the French would retire to the coast and begin military action about April 20.[6]

Meanwhile the government of Mexico had been actively preparing for the advent of hostilities. Juárez addressed the nation, denouncing whatever pretext the invading nations might have to wage war on Mexico, and summoning all Mexicans to the defense of their country.[7]Although most of the interior states were still having internal troubles, they sent contingents of troops to the capital. Some of the Conservative leaders, out of a spirit of nationalism, offered their services to the government; but the major reactionary leaders, Mejía, Márquez, and Zuloaga, continued to oppose national forces and generally aided the cause of the intervention.

González Ortega, who had been in the field with the troops in pursuit of Márquez, returned to Zacatecas in November, 1861, to take over the governorship of the state and to raise funds and men for the army. By the last of December there were about 5,000 men under his command, and the state was the scene of feverish preparations for the anticipated war with the European powers.[8]At the beginning of 1862 martial law was declared in the states of Puebla, San Luis Potosí, Veracruz, and Tamaulipas. Doblado appointed González Ortega as military commander of San Luis Potosí, with instructions to keep order in the state and prepare its defenses.[9]González Ortega's command soon was expanded to include all the forces of San Luis Potosí, Zacatecas, and Aguascalientes.[10]

For the next few months González Ortega remained in Zacatecas and San Luis Potosí raising troops and money. In San Luis Potosí he was faced with the task of protecting the royalist residents from mobs angered over the intervention. In line with the policy set forth by Juárez, González Ortega treated the Spanish kindly and promised them protection. In his effort to raise funds for the government he once again turned to the churches as a source of wealth. The "Devil Preacher" of the Reform was still convinced that churches must be made subservient to civil authorities and their wealth used for the benefit of the nation.[11]

González Ortega kept the national government posted on activities in the states of the interior, and he also kept in contact with Juárez and some of the members of the cabinet. He assured Juárez that the country had faith in the president's ability to settle affairs with the foreign powers without sacrificing the honor of Mexico. He also expressed the hope that actual fighting could be avoided.[12]Finally, on May 19, 1862, González Ortega started for Mexico City at the head of his forces.[13] On May 31, while he was on his way to the national capital, the congress declared him constitutional president of the Supreme Court as a result of elections held during the last months of 1861.[14]This was probably no surprise to anyone since he had been serving in an interim capacity for some months and was still one of the most popular figures in Mexico.

Meanwhile, in April, 1862, hostilities began between the French and Mexicans. On April 20 the French, under the leadership of General Charles Laurencez, occupied Orizaba, ignoring their obligation to return to the coast before commencing hostilities. General Almonte, who had returned to Mexico under French auspices, issued a proclamation to the Mexican people urging support of the intervention, and some areas under clerical influence declared for Almonte as chief of the republic. Shortly thereafter, a French declaration named Almonte as supreme chief of the nation and the French forces began to move toward the capital some 150 miles away.

The first objective of the French was the city of Puebla, about halfway between Orizaba and Mexico City. The city was defended by a Mexican force under Ignacio Zaragoza, and Laurencez made the mistake of expecting an easy victory. On May 5 he launched an attack against the unskilled Mexican soldiers, who decisively defeated the French army. Zaragoza and Porfirio Díaz, a subordinate officer at Puebla, won fame for themselves and Mexico. The anniversary of this battle became one of the great national holidays in Mexico.[15]Zaragoza now made plans to push the French back to the coast from Orizaba, to which point they had retreated following their defeat at Puebla. His forces were strengthened by the arrival of González Ortega's army from Mexico City.[16]

Shortly after his arrival on the scene, González Ortega took it upon himself to seek some way to avoid further hostilities. On June 10 he wrote to French Minister de Saligny and proposed an armistice to establish diplomatic relations. González Ortega explained that Mexico was pro-republican and would not tolerate a monarchy. He very naively asked if it would not look better in the future if the issues at stake were settled by diplomacy rather than war.[17]Although this action was taken without the consent of Juárez or Zaragoza, González Ortega at least communicated his actions to Juárez.[18]Juárez very politely advised him to confine himself to military operations and leave diplomatic matters to those in authority. He further voiced the hope that González Ortega's peace feeler had not hindered the operations against the French. Temporarily subdued and having received no answer from Saligny, González Ortega assured Juárez that the proposal had been made in strict confidence and would not embarrass the general-in-chief or the supreme government.[19]

While this exchange of letters was taking place, Zaragoza had planned an attack on Orizaba for June 14. González Ortega was assigned the task of taking and holding the heights of Borrego overlooking the city so as to prevent the French from gaining this vantage point when the main Mexican army attacked. González Ortega carried out his orders on schedule, but within a few hours the French surprised his exhausted forces and decisively defeated them in the battle which followed. González Ortega explained the defeat on the exhaustion of his men and the element of surprise, which had resulted from the "criminal imprudence" of the officer responsible for the guard.[20]Whether this

69

explanation was correct or not, the defeat was costly for the Mexicans. Zaragoza, ignorant of the defeat at Borrego, launched his attack as planned but failed to take Orizaba. Zaragoza then retired to Ingenio, Puebla, where he remained for some time. The French failed to pursue their advantage and returned to Orizaba.[21]González Ortega, following his defeat at Borrego, retreated to Jésus María and thence to Tehuacan in the state of Puebla.[22]

For the next few months there was little military activity. The French concentrated on fortifying Orizaba and their other gains along the coast. The failure of the French armies thus far, and the lack of expected support from large numbers of Mexicans, caused repercussions in France. Napoleon, however, was too deeply involved by this time to withdraw, and 30,000 soldiers were dispatched for Mexico under the command of General Frederic Forey, who was to replace Laurencez.[23]

The Mexican government continued its efforts to meet the financial needs of the war. Among the measures it imposed were new property taxes and forced loans. In August, 1862, Doblado, in a move which caused some surprise, resigned from the cabinet. Within a few days Juan Antonio de la Fuente took Doblado's post, and Doblado assumed command of the forces operating in the interior against Mejia.[24]Another personnel change was necessary on September 8, 1862, when General Zaragoza died of typhoid fever. In view of González Ortega's recent defeat at Borrego, there was some surprise when he was named to succeed Zaragoza as head of the army of the west, but later events were to prove that the appointment was well considered. It had the immediate effect of silencing the talk of his possible disloyalty to the Juárez government.

González Ortega immediately set to work building up the defenses around the city of Puebla. He required all able-bodied men between the ages of fourteen and sixty to work on the fortifications one day each week or to pay an amount considered to be the equivalent. González Ortega supervised this work personally, and on occasion joined in the manual labor to raise the morale of the populace.[26]To aid the national cause in a financial way, González Ortega added weight to the laws providing for the alienation of funds and property belonging to the Church by an order that all who obstructed these laws would be judged and sentenced as traitors.[27]By November, although the work on the fortifications continued, González Ortega believed that Puebla was almost invincible and would serve as a center of Mexican operations.[28]

González Ortega's loyalty to the republican cause was tested in November by an exchange of letters with the new French Commander Frederic Forey. He had sent Forey several wounded French soldiers captured in the May 5 battle, along with a zouave's medal taken in the same engagement. Forey expressed gratitude and stated that he had received González Ortega's letter as from a brave soldier, but that he could not correspond with the government of Mexico without repugnance. He also expressed the wish that González Ortega's sword might serve a better cause in the near future.[29]González Ortega forwarded the contents of these letters to Juárez, who advised him to answer that he considered Forey insulting — not to the person of Juárez, but to the government of Mexico. Juárez listed some points which González Ortega might make in his reply to Forey[30]

González Ortega complied. On November 16, 1862, he informed Forey that regardless of the results of the military events the French would have to treat with Mexico's chief magistrate, whose powers came from the nation. He added that France's true interests did not lie in cooperating with a few discontented persons to overthrow a government sustained by the Mexican people. As for himself, aside from his personal regard for Juárez, he wished Forey to understand that he was freely serving his country as an independent citizen. He concluded by returning Forey's letter, stating that it had no place among his records.[31]

At Puebla the work on the defenses continued. On December 10, 1862, González Ortega ordered the evacuation of several religious convents in the city with the alleged humanitarian object of keeping the monks from undergoing the terrors of a siege. A more practical reason became apparent on December 26, when another decree ordered the occupation of these monasteries, which were among the strongest and highest buildings in the area, for defense purposes.[32]

In the meantime, a plan for the defense of Mexico had been prepared. If the French attacked Puebla, González Ortega would direct operations while Ignacio Comonfort's army of the center supported him from outside the city. If, instead, the French launched an attack against Mexico City, Comonfort would direct operations while González Ortega's army would act in the supporting role. In either event the two armies were to operate independently.[33] During the last months of 1862 González Ortega was stricken with a fever which occasionally confined him to bed, but he evidently was not sufficiently ill to turn the command over to someone else.[34] The military plans remained unchanged, and González Ortega continued preparations for the defense of Puebla.

In February Juárez visited Puebla, now renamed Puebla de Zaragoza, to review the army and inspect the fortifications. Shortly thereafter Forey began to move against the city. González Ortega declared martial law on March 10, and four days later he invited all families to leave the town as soon as possible. Fighting between besiegers and besieged began on March 21. The Mexican forces at Puebla numbered about 22,000 men, while the French force consisted of over 26,000.[35] After the initial French attacks, which were generally unsuccessful, the siege resolved into a stubborn battle in which the French gained a little ground each day and the Mexicans resisted bravely every inch of the way.[36]

On April 14 González Ortega dispatched several officers and a small detachment of soldiers to make their way through the besieging forces and report to Comonfort and Juárez on the needs of the army in Puebla. But no aid for the besieged city arrived, and González Ortega's officers could not return for they were re-assigned to the army of the center under Comonfort. At about the same time Comonfort, who according to the defense plan was to operate in conjunction with González Ortega from outside the city, asked him to send 5,000 men. González Ortega could not meet this request, for he needed all of his men to defend the city. Comonfort evidently failed to carry out his part in the defense of Puebla throughout the siege, for he lacked military ability and he was determined to act independently of González Ortega.

On various occasions some of González Ortega's officers urged him to abandon the plaza of Puebla while there was still a chance to save the army, but on each occasion he succeeded in encouraging them to hold out a little longer. Throughout the siege he remained confident of victory, and his confidence infected the defending forces.

On April 25 González Ortega wrote to Comonfort that the city could hold out for eight more days without relief. On April 29 he declared that it was time to try to break the siege and again asked for Comonfort's aid. Comonfort promised that a convoy of supplies would be forthcoming and that Puebla should be held. Although there was nothing left in the city that could be utilized for food but the horses, mules, and dogs, the assurance that supplies were on the way encouraged the defenders to hold on.

The faint hope that the siege might yet be broken doomed any French attempt to arrange a capitulation. On May 7, during an exchange of prisoners, General Forey and Colonel Juan Togno, an aide of González Ortega, held a conference. The French commander spoke of the uselessness of further defense, which, he said, would be carrying things beyond military necessity and would appear to be only for the purpose of winning personal fame. He assured Togno that González Ortega had won fame already, and he expressed willingness to grant honorable terms of capitulation. Forey also offered González Ortega the support of the French army if he desired to make himself president of Mexico. This appeal to González Ortega's presidential ambitions failed, however, for he instructed his aide to say that since they involved French intervention in Mexican affairs, the proposals could not be considered. He also refused to participate in a conference suggested by Forey.

On May 8 the garrison at Puebla heard firing in the direction of San Lorenzo, and assumed that this was the expected attempt by Comonfort to supply the city, although there had been no hint that the move might occur from that direction. The defenders of the city remained uncertain until the following afternoon, when they learned by letter from Forey of Comonfort's defeat at San Lorenzo. The army of the center, in attempting to conduct a train into Puebla, had been routed and driven back in retreat.[37]

Now that all hope of aid was gone, González Ortega wrote to Comonfort advising him that on May 14 the army in Puebla would attempt to break the siege. Comonfort was to distract the French with an attack in another direction. Comonfort did not reply by the appointed date, however, and the attempted break was not made. The city held out for two more days until, with virtually no ammunition or food left, a conference of officers decided that González Ortega should attempt to arrange terms of capitulation. Forey insisted on unconditional surrender. Another council of war on May 17 decided to destroy all the armament in the city and to hoist the white flag.[38]When this was done Forey was informed that the Mexican officers awaited his pleasure in the palace. He asked the officers to sign paroles placing them on their honor as prisoners, but they refused.

The siege of Puebla, though it ended in a French victory, was not a humiliating defeat for Mexico. The historian José M. Vigil has summed up the action in these words: "After a siege of sixty-two days the valiant defenders of Puebla succumbed, not to the arms of a powerful enemy but to the horrors of hunger and the lack of munitions of war. A town had been lost, but the honor of Mexico had been saved."[39]

The defense of Puebla was celebrated not only in Mexico

but throughout the world. The London *Times, La Iberia* of Madrid, and even *Le Temps* of Paris commented favorably on the heroic defense of the city.[40]One observer, writing after the event, compared the defense of Puebla to the famous sieges of Strasburg and Metz.[41]Although later writers have questioned González Ortega's military ability or have blamed Comonfort or Juárez for the defeat, most accounts of the event praise the Mexican defenders.[42]

Following the surrender of Puebla, the Mexican field and company grade officers were marched on foot and unarmed to Veracruz, with González Ortega and the other captured generals following in closely guarded carriages.[43]During the trip González Ortega learned that the French had committed various outrages against the prisoners. These French actions increased his desire to escape and continue the war, and at Orizaba he saw an opportunity.[44]On May 27 González Ortega, Llave, Prieto, Patoni, Díaz, and other generals escaped from the former convent of San José de García by means of disguises obtained from dealers who had been authorized to sell the prisoners provisions. The French guards were unaware of the importance of their prisoners, and their ignorance made the escape possible.[45]

When the news of the fall of Puebla reached Mexico City Juárez placed the district under stringent martial law and accepted Comonfort's resignation of his command. He called for additional forces, and made plans to defend the capital. It soon became apparent that the city could not be held, however, and the congress ordered the chief federal authorities to transfer their activities to San Luis Potosí, at the same time granting the president extraordinary powers for the duration of the emergency.[46]Juárez, accompanied by most of the public officials, left the capital on May 31, 1863.[47]On arriving in San Luis Potosí he issued a proclamation setting forth the reasons for abandoning the capital, and he sent circulars authorizing the state governors to act in certain cases without instructions from the federal government.[48]

Following his escape from the French, González Ortega,

accompanied by Llave and Patoni, made his way through Huatusco and Jalapa to Tezuitlan in Puebla, where he arrived at the end of May. From there he went by way of Pachuca, Hidalgo, to Guanajuato, where on June 12, 1863 he conferred with Doblado.[49] González Ortega wrote his wife that he and his companions had been received with enthusiasm wherever they stopped.[50]

González Ortega's reaction to his journey probably changed a little a few days later on the journey from Guanajuato to San Luis Potosi. Near the hacienda of Quemada in San Luis Potosi, González Ortega asked Llave to help him carry part of the 500 ounces of gold which had been taken from Puebla. During the transfer, some of the gold fell to the ground in sight of the soldiers Doblado had supplied as an escort. The soldiers, who were following behind the three generals, plotted to kill the three officers and sieze the gold. Llave, who fell behind González Ortega and Patoni, was caught by surprise and shot in the back. He managed to shout a warning to them, and the speed of their horses enabled them to escape.[51]

González Ortega continued on to San Luis Potosí, where he expected to take up his duties as president of the supreme court. In July, however, he assumed the governorship of Zacatecas, which had been placed under a state of siege because of the French advance. Whether he could legally hold this state office and serve as president of the court was to become a debatable matter. The historian Niceto de Zamacois accused Juárez of placing González Ortega in charge of Zacatecas and then, in a little more than year, declaring that in accepting a state office González Ortega had forfeited his position on the court by violating the constitution.[52] There is no evidence that Juárez made the appointment, but there is also no evidence that the constitutional question had even been raised before. It would appear that later events made the question crucial, and that if there were doubts when González Ortega accepted the governorship, they were conveniently ignored.

The long flight of the Mexican government had begun, a

flight which would not end until the final victory over the French in 1867. The Mexican army, disorganized though it was, had still not been destroyed; and despite the intervention there were still political questions to be settled. In addition there was González Ortega, who though once defeated, was not through with his struggle against the French.

NOTES

1. D y L, *Legislación,* IX, 243-245.
2. William Spence Robertson, "The Tripartite Treaty of London," The *Hispanic American Historical Review,* (hereafter cited as *HAHR),* XX (May, 1940), 167-189, presents a full discussion of these events.
3. Zamacona was named to this post on July 13, 1861, in a cabinet revision. Others named at that time were Blas Balcárcel, *Fomento;* Joaquín Ruiz, Justice; Zaragoza, War; and Higinio Núñez, Treasury. Ruiz was to direct the department of *Gobernación* temporarily. Bancroft, *Mexico,* VI, 18.
4. Under this agreement previous conventions were declared to be in force and new debts were also recognized. Great Britain was to have inspectors in the maritime custom houses and was also to have the right to examine the books of those houses. The text of this treaty appears in Antonio de la Peña y Reves, *La labor diplomática de D. Manuel María de Zamacona como Secretario de Relaciones Exteriores* (Archivo Histórico Diplomático Mexicano, Series 2, No. 28), 97-100, as well as *El Heraldo,* November 29, 1861.
5. The new ministry was constituted as follows: Doblado, Foreign Relations and *Gobernación;* Jesús Terán, Justice; González Echeverría, Treasury; Zaragoza, War (until December 25, when he was succeeded by Pedro Hinojosa); Doblado, *Fomento* (until December 16, when the department was merged with that of Justice). Bancroft, *Mexico,* VI, 26.
6. This account of the background to the intervention and its first phases has been based primarily on the accounts of Egon Caesar Count Corti, *Maximilian and Charlotte of Mexico* (New York, 1928, 2 vols.), I, 98-176, and Roeder, *Juárez,* I, II, 318-423. The invading troops had been moved to La Soledad to escape the unhealthful climate along the coast.

7. D y L, *Legislación,* IX, 344-346.
8. *El Siglo XIX,* November 16 and December 21, 1861.
9. Doblado to González Ortega, México, January 2, 1862, in González Ortega Typescripts, V; *El Siglo XIX,* January 7, 1862.
10. *El Siglo XIX,* January 24, 1862; Zamacois, *Historia de Méjico,* XVI, 26-27.
11. *El Siglo XIX,* January 10 and 25, March 28, April 26, May 1, 1862; Primo Feliciano Velázquez, *Historia de San Luis Potosí* (México, 1948, 4 vols.), III, 355-356. A letter from González Ortega to Satero de la Torre, the *jefe político* of Nieves, Zacatecas, December 6, 1861, in *El Siglo XIX,* January 15, 1862, contains a fairly detailed expression of González Ortega's belief in the separation of church and state and the observance of the reform laws concerning religion.
12. González Ortega to Juárez, San Luis Potosí, March 4, 1862, in Archivo Juárez Manuscripts; González Ortega to Jesús Terán, San Luis Potosí, March 11, 1862, in Jesús Terán Correspondence Typescripts (University of Texas).
13. Juan Hidalgo to Comonfort, San Luis Potosí, May 15, 1862, and José Manuel Aguirre to Comonfort, San Luis Potosí, May 19, 1862, in Ignacio Comonfort Manuscripts (University of Texas).
14. D y L, *Legislación,* IX, 472-473. The issues of *El Siglo XIX* in October, November and December, 1861, carry scattered returns of this election.
15. Corti, *Maximilian and Charlotte,* I, 176; Vigil, *Reforma,* pp. 531-538.
16. *El Siglo XIX,* June 2, 1862.
17. González Ortega to Saligny, Palmar, June 10, 1862, in Archivo Juárez Manuscripts.
18. González Ortega to Juárez, Palmar, June 10, 1862, in *ibid.*
19. Juárez to González Ortega, México, June 13, 1862, and González Ortega to Juárez, Palmar, June 17, 1862, in *ibid.*
20. Official Report of the Battle of Borrego by General González Ortega, Jesús María, June 14, 1862, in Matías Romero (ed.), *Correspondenica de la legación mexicana en Washington durante la intervención extranjera, 1860-1868* (México, 1870-1892, 10 vols.), II, 1181-1183. This work will be cited hereafter as *Méx. Leg. Corresp.* See also *U. S. House Executive Documents,* 37 Cong., 3 Sess., (1862-1863), No. 54, 147.
21. Official Report by Zaragoza, Ingenio, June 14, 1862, in *El Siglo XIX,* June 17, 1862.
22. Manuel Rivera Cambas, *Los gobernantes de México* (México, 1873, 2 vols.), II, 632. Cambas also states that González Ortega spent most

of his time at Tehuacan doing nothing but writing poetry.
23. Corti, *Maximilian and Charlotte*, I, 177-180; Bancroft, *Mexico*, VI, 54-55.
24. *El Heraldo*, August 15, 1862; Vigil, *Reforma*, p. 559. It has been suggested that Doblado was asked to resign because of the suspicion that he was willing to do away with Juárez and compromise the principles of the Constitution of 1857 in order to avoid further hostilities. Bancroft, *Mexico*, VI, 53. A letter from José M. Patoni to Esteban Ávila, Durango, January 31, 1862, in Doblado Typescripts, mentions a rumor along this line.
25. Rivera, *Anales*, p. 97. There were at this time three Mexican armies, the army of the east under González Ortega; the army of the interior under Doblado, and the army of the center under Comonfort, who had been allowed to re-enter Mexico several months earlier. See Zayas Enríquez, *Juárez*, p. 163, and Roeder, *Juárez*, II, 489-493, for comments on the appointment of González Ortega.
26. Galindo y Galindo, *Gran década*, II, 342-343.
27. Zamacois, *Historia de Méjico*, XVI, 288-289. See also González Ortega to Terán, Palmar, September 1, 1862, in Terán Typescripts.
28. González Ortega to Fuente, Zaragoza, November 8, 1862, in Comonfort Manuscripts.
29. Forey to González Ortega, Orizaba, November 10, 1862, in Archivo Juárez Manuscripts, and *Mex. Leg. Corresp.*, III, 96.
30. Telegram and letter from González Ortega to Juárez, Puebla, November 12, 1862; Juárez to González Ortega, Mexico, November 13, 1862; telegram from González Ortega to Juárez, Puebla, November 14, 1862, in Archivo Juárez Manuscripts.
31. González Ortega to Forey, Zaragoza, November 16, 1862, in *Mex. Leg. Corresp.*, III, 96-97. On November 17, 1862, Minister of War Blanco communicated Juárez' approval of his actions to González Ortega. *Ibid.*, 97-98.
32. Zamacois, *Historia de Méjico*, XVI, 306-307.
33. González Ortega had requested that the command be unified under either himself or Comonfort depending upon whether the attack was made on Puebla or Mexico City. Minister of War Blanco had decided in favor of independent armies supporting one another. *Parte general que da al supremo gobierno de la nación respecto de la defensa de la plaza de Zaragoza el C. general Jesús González Ortega* (México, 1871), pp. 7-11. This official report by González Ortega on the siege of Puebla was issued on September 16, 1863, in Zacatecas. It will be cited hereafter as *Parte general*.
34. Vicente Riva Palacio to González Ortega, Tehuacan, February 12,

1863, in *El Diario Oficial,* February 18, 1863; González Ortega to Fuente, Zaragoza, November 8, 1862, and March 6, 1863; in Genero García (ed.), "El Sitio de Puebla en 1863 según los archivos de D. Ignacio Comonfort y de D. Juan Antonio de la Fuente," in *Documentos inéditos o muy raros para la historia de México,* XXIII, 1.

35. *Diario Oficial,* March 10, 1863; Bancroft, *Mexico,* VI, 62.

36. The account of the siege given here follows for the most part that given in *Parte general, passim.* This report appears to be reasonably accurate and unprejudiced, although it is obvious that González Ortega was reluctant to expose any of his own mistakes. Much of the correspondence relative to this event will be found in García (ed.) "El Sitio de Puebla," and in the issues of *Diario Oficial* for that period. See also Vigil, *Reforma,* pp. 574-581, and Zamacois, *Historia de Méjico,* XVI, 369-465.

37. Forey to González Ortega, May 9, 1863, in *Parte general,* pp. 166-168.

38. General order of May 17, 1863, and González Ortega to Minister of War, Zaragoza, May 17, 1863, in *ibid.,* pp. 197-201.

39. Vigil, *Reforma,* p. 581.

40. Zayas Enríquez, *Juárez,* pp. 166-167; Galindo y Galindo, *Gran década,* II, 556.

41. Cited in Galindo y Galindo, *Gran década,* II, 555.

42. Almost any work on the intervention comments at some length on this battle and several writers have argued at great length on where the blame for the defeat should lie. Francisco Bulnes, in his *El verdadero Juárez y la verdad sobre la intervención y el imperio* (México, 1904), pp. 189-190, asserts that González Ortega was a stupid military man and that the defense of Puebla was simply based on the earlier May 5 battle at that city, a fact which in itself was stupid. Porfirio Díaz in his *Memorias,* I, 276-277, 315-316, points out that González Ortega should have attacked the French at the very beginning of the siege and he would have been successful, but Díaz admits that by May, 1863, the situation was impossible. González Ortega, *Golpe,* pp. 111-141, points out the various mistakes which he feels Comonfort and Juárez made in not aiding him and intimates that perhaps Juárez did not want him to gain any more fame than he already had.

It would appear to be enough to establish that the defense of Puebla was acclaimed and that González Ortega acquitted himself well throughout the siege. It is apparent that there was a need for more coordination between the Mexican armies, but even if this had existed there is no reason to assume that Comonfort would have been successful in relieving the city.

43. González Ortega to Severo Cosío, Zaragoza, May 21, 1863, in González Ortega Typescripts, V. González Ortega's son and wife were evidently with him during the siege of Puebla, since they were to stay in that city when the French moved the prisoners toward the coast.
44. *Parte general,* pp. 217-220.
45. Dispatch from Forey to Minister of War, no date, in *U.S. House Executive Documents,* 39 Cong., 1 Sess. (1865-1866), No. 73, Part 1, 218; Rivera, *Anales,* p. 104. See also Vigil, *Reforma,* p. 584.
46. *El Siglo XIX,* May 29, 1863.
47. Bancroft, *Mexico,* VI, 71-72.
48. D y L, *Legislación,* IX, 623-625. A cabinet reorganization also took place at this time. The cabinet by September 10 was composed of Lerdo, José M. Iglesias, Núñez and Comonfort. Bancroft, *México,* VI, 72.
49. Galindo y Galindo, *Gran década,* II, 606-608; Rivera, *Anales,* p. 107; Zamacois, *Historia de Méjico,* XVI, 479.
50. González Ortega to his wife, June 13, 1863, in González Ortega, *Golpe,* pp. 144-145.
51. Rivera, *Anales,* p. 109. The date usually given for this incident is June 14, but González Ortega, *Golpe,* p. 145, insisted that this was incorrect, although he was not certain of the correct one. Certainly the event took place a few days following the departure from Guanajuato. It has been suggested that the soldiers involved had fought under González Ortega earlier and did not really wish to kill him. Juárez to Viduarri, San Luis Potosí, June 22, 1863, in S. Roel (ed.), *Correspondencia particular de D. Santiago Vidaurri* (Monterrey, 1946), pp. 203-204.
52. Zamacois, *Historia de Méjico,* XVI, 626; Lerdo to González Ortega, San Luis Potosí, November 30, 1864, in *Mex. Leg. Corresp.,* IV, 561-565. Zayas Enríquez, *Juárez,* p. 187, states that this assumption of state power was without the permission of Juárez.

VI
González Ortega's Hegira

Following the victory at Puebla the French moved into Mexico City early in June, 1863. After staging a welcome for the conquering forces, Forey selected a supreme council of thirty-five members which then named a governing board of three men headed by Almonte and called a convention of 215 "notables" to determine the permanent form of government. On July 8 the convention pronounced itself in favor of establishing a monarchy and sent a delegation to offer the crown of Mexico to Archduke Maximilian of Austria. Maximilian demanded a plebiscite to determine the wishes of the Mexican people. The election seemed desirable to Napoleon III for the possible effect it might have on diplomatic relations with other nations, and the campaign to win an expression of approval for Maximilian began.

While these political steps were being taken the French tried to consolidate their military gains. By the first of August they held more than sixty towns and hamlets between Veracruz and Mexico City and controlled a circuit of about twenty-five leagues around the capital. Two months later the French holdings remained about the same, and there was fighting in all of the central provinces from Jalisco and San Luis Potosí to Oaxaca.[1]

Before the end of the rainy season, which had thus far prevented any concerted drive, the French forces underwent a change of command. Forey and Saligny, whose dual control of the French forces had proven slow and unsatisfactory, were recalled, and General F. A. Bazaine assumed control of the French armies. The new commander reorganized his forces, and by the beginning of November they numbered about 34,700 men with 14,000 of these mobilized to begin operations as soon as the weather permitted.[2]

In the face of the French occupation of the center of the country, Juárez exerted himself to the limit to maintain his government and obtain funds to sustain his armies. It was easy enough to find men to fight the French, but supplying them was difficult. Differences of opinion arose within the Cabinet over management of affairs, and on September 1 Juárez organized a new cabinet.[3] At the same time he also instituted a military reorganization in an attempt to restore unity to the disorganized Republican army. He divided the army into five divisions under the direction of Minister of War Comonfort. He placed the eastern division, consisting of about 3,000 men, under Porfirio Díaz, while a second division of more than 4,000 men was placed under Doblado's command at Guanajuato. Other divisions of about the same size were commanded by José López Uraga in Michoacan and González Ortega in Zacatecas. General Berriozábal assumed command of a reserve division.[4]

In addition to his military problems, Juárez also faced a political crisis. On November 28, 1863, while still at San Luis Potosí, he had exercised the extraordinary powers conferred on him by congress in May to declare that the terms of the existing magistrates of the supreme court expired in December, and that since it was impossible to hold an election, he would name replacements. This meant that González Ortega would be the only elected member of the court still serving, since his term ran until June, 1868. Following this decree, Juárez announced that he would name his appointees even before the expiration date of the terms of the incumbents.[5]

Some Liberal leaders resented this exercise of dictatorial powers, for they felt that Juárez had violated the constitutional separation of powers. Opponents of Juárez, who were motivated by jealousy and rivalry, emphasized the government's military reverses in an effort to discredit the chief executive. A climax was reached on January 14, 1864, when a commission representing González Ortega, Doblado, and Governor J. María Chávez of Aguascalientes, asked Juárez to resign as president.[6] Their purported reason for demanding his resignation was that the French claimed they would not treat with Juárez. The commissioners assured Juárez that whatever his decision was, it would be obeyed. He refused the request and pointed out that the quarrel of the French was not with him personally but with the form of government. In addition Juárez asserted that as an elected official it was his duty to remain in office.[7]

In stating to Doblado his reasons for not resigning, Juárez added that there was no assurance that the enemy would treat with González Ortega, for they considered him a man who had gone back on his word. Juárez doubted, in fact, that the French would treat with any Mexican who opposed the intervention.[8]

The firmness of Juárez prevailed over the wishes of Doblado and González Ortega. On January 25 González Ortega wrote to Juárez that he intended to remain loyal to the government, and on January 27 he issued a proclamation calling upon the people of Zacatecas to continue fighting the French and to exert themselves to the utmost in the conflict.[9] In view of González Ortega's attitude it is difficult to understand the reasoning behind the request for Juárez resignation. It would appear that he honestly believed that he could get terms from the French when Juárez could not. At the same time Juárez was probably correct in assuming that the French would not treat with any president who would not accept the intervention. How far González Ortega would have gone in that direction is not clear, although it is certain that he wished to end the fighting as soon as possible. Whatever his motive, his actions in this instance were subject to censure.[10]

During November and December, 1863, the fighting went against the Republican forces. Querétaro and Morelia fell to the French in November, and shortly thereafter San Miguel Allende, Guanajuato, León and Lagos also came under French control. The French successes endangered San Luis Potosí, and on December 22 Juárez and his government abandoned that city and moved north to Saltillo, capital of Coahuila.[11]

Still the French advance continued. Bazaine occupied Guadalajara on January 7, and at the end of the month Mejía seized Matehuala in San Luis Potosí. In February González Ortega abandoned Zacatecas and moved his capital north to Fresnillo. The French soon occupied Fresnillo, and González Ortega's forces retreated to Sain Alto, Sombrerete, and other points in the north of the state as circumstances required. While located in this area González Ortega collected tribute from the mines and awaited the opportunity for some effective demonstration against the French.[12]

In the middle of March Juárez called on González Ortega for aid because of continued trouble with Santiago Vidaurri in Neuvo León. Through his Minister of Finance Juárez had demanded that the sources of revenue in the states controlled by Vidaurri be turned over to the federal government. Vidaurri declared that the states could not spare these revenues and forbade the customshouse collectors to transfer any funds to Juárez. The latter replied by announcing that he planned to move the federal government to Vidaurri's capital at Monterrey. Juárez entered Monterrey on February 12, accompanied by troops under Doblado, but with the approach of additional troops loyal to Vidaurri, he retired within two days. In an effort to restore the prestige of the government, Juárez called upon Doblado, González Ortega, and others to aid in bringing Vidaurri under control.[13]

González Ortega at first suggested that he might be able to retake Zacatecas from the French if he moved in that direction rather than against Vidaurri. Both Juárez and Lerdo repeated the need for aid and voiced the belief that the French forces were too numerous for an attack to be successful.[14] As a result González Ortega turned his forces toward Saltillo to join Doblado, Patoni, and others. Before he reached Saltillo, however, the need for aid had passed. Vidaurri, seeing that Juárez was imperiling his private little empire, entered into negotations with Bazaine. Juárez issued a decree dissolving the union of Coahuila and Nuevo León and declared them in a state of siege. His gathering forces caused some defection among Vidaurri's supporters, and the latter attempted to reach an agreement with the president. When Juárez demanded unconditional surrender, Vidaurri abandoned Monterrey and fled to Texas.[15] Juárez then occupied Monterrey while the republican forces checked the French temporarily at San Luis Potosí.

As the time approached for Maximilian to take the throne of Mexico, which he had accepted at Miramar on April 10, 1864, the ground held by the imperialist forces had increased considerably.[16] The most important part of the country had been brought under their control, although republican guerrillas still operated in many areas including Michoacán, Jalisco, and southern Puebla. To the north the republicans held the sparsely inhabited provinces of Sinaloa, Sonora, Durango, Chihuahua, Nuevo León, and part of Tamaulipas. In the south they occupied Guerrero, Oaxaca, Tabasco, and Chiapas, where Porfirio Díaz had been unusually successful in keeping the French at bay.[17]

Maximilian and Charlotte landed at Veracruz on May 28, 1864, and proceeded by easy stages to Mexico City, where on June 12 the monarchical party received them with enthusiasm. Maximilian soon demonstrated that his policy was to be one of conciliation and he made overtures to Juárez and the other Liberals, indicating a desire to harmonize the opposing factions. This policy did not win favor with many Mexicans. The reactionary elements disapproved of it, and the republicans saw in Maximilian's presence nothing but an odious monarchy under a foreign prince. Juárez quickly rejected Maximilian's overtures and continued plans to drive the French from the country.[18]

While Maximilian was establishing his empire in the capital, the French continued to win it for him in the north. On August 15, 1864, Juárez was forced to abandon Monterrey, and in September the government moved to Nazas, Durango, and then to the town of Chihuahua on October 15. Doblado and other republican leaders fled to the United States in August, either because they felt that the situation in Mexico was hopeless or because they hoped to serve the republican cause better abroad. Juárez himself sent his wife and children to the United States to insure their safety.[19]

During the government's long migration González Ortega, who commanded the forces in Aguascalientes, San Luis Potosí, Zacatecas, Durango, Chihuahua, and Coahuila, continued to fight a delaying action.[20] On September 21, at Majoma in the state of Durango, he attacked the French and was defeated in a bloody engagement. This defeat, which was extremely costly to the republicans, has been called the last stand of their armies in the north.[21] González Ortega received considerable criticism for the defeat. Juárez, writing to his son-in-law in the United States, stated that the defeat came when González Ortega had all the advantages, because he "did not engage all his forces but only a small part, which fought heroically, and the other, which was the larger, remained drawn up and retired in order" without firing a shot. The worst thing, Juárez said, was that González Ortega allowed his forces to disband when they had gotten ten leagues from the enemy without being pursued.[22]

González Ortega offered no rebuttal to Juárez' claim that all the troops did not participate in the battle. He did, however, explain that the "heat of conflict, physical prostration, engendered through privation and the march through the desert had so far worn out the national troops" that he ordered a retreat. He insisted, furthermore, that no amount of discipline would have prevented the disbanding of the forces, since the soldiers felt that they had done their duty and could now serve best in detached bodies.[23]

Following the defeat at Majoma, González Ortega apparently operated with small forces in the north before retiring to Chihuahua to await developments.[24] While in Chihuahua on November 30, 1864, he addressed a letter to Minister Lerdo asking for an interpretation of the constitution with regard to the date on which Juárez' term of office expired. Under Article 79 of the constitution, in the absence of an elected president, the president of the supreme court was to serve as chief executive until elections could be held. For this reason, González Ortega stated, his position as president of the court compelled him to inquire into the matter.[25] The problem arose from the fact that Juárez had assumed office in May, 1861, rather than December. The constitution simply stated that the president's term was to begin on December 1 and to last for four years.[26] Juárez might give up his office in December, 1865, giving him a term six months longer than that provided in the constitution. Lerdo replied on the same day and pointed out that under article 80 of the constitution the chief executive would serve until the last day of November of the fourth year following his election. By this interpretation Juárez' term did not expire until December, 1865. González Ortega accepted this interpretation, as he had indicated that he would, and he said nothing more on the subject at that time.[27]

In the same exchange of letters González Ortega requested and received an answer with regard to his legal right to hold the position of president of the supreme court and the governorship of Zacatecas at the same time. According to Article 118 of the constitution, no person could exercise two elective positions in the government simultaneously, but the person concerned might select the position which he preferred.[28] Lerdo told him that, as the government had many times informed him, he should make a choice between the two positions. He added that González Ortega apparently preferred the governorship of Zacatecas, or so his actions indicated. Lerdo went on to say, however, that under the circumstances and in view of the impossibility of providing for a successor to the presidency, González Ortega was still considered as the one who would become president in the event that the office were vacated.[29]

For the next month, González Ortega remained in Chihuahua without instructions from the government and without performing any official functions either civil or military.[30] During this time he reached the decision that he could aid the republican cause most by leaving Mexico and entering the country at some other point where he might be able to engage in combat again. In addition, either because of fear for his own life or because of the influence of friends, he decided to proceed to some area which was not under Juárez' direct influence. While there is no reason to assume that his life was actually in danger at this time, it certainly was not comfortable for a man of his ambition to be so completely under the control of Juárez. On December 28, at any rate, he wrote to Juárez requesting permission to proceed to the interior of Mexico to aid the republican cause. At the same time he requested permission to leave Mexico if necessary and to reenter the country at some other point.[31]

Juárez approved the request and instructed the Minister of War to supply González Ortega with the necessary papers. In the official reply from the Minister of War, González Ortega was granted permission "as President of the Supreme Court of Justice to pass to points not occupied by the enemy" in order to continue defending the independence of Mexico. This permission was granted "for an indefinite time, until you present yourself at the residence of the government or until the government recalls you or gives you some commission." González Ortega was given authority to go directly, by sea or through foreign territory, to some other part of the republic.[32]

Once he received permission he began to make plans for his departure from the country, but the journey was delayed until January 29 because of heavy snows in northern Mexico. On February 17, 1865, however, he had reached Paso del Norte, and a month later he was in Santa Fe, New Mexico. From Santa Fe he went to St. Louis, Missouri, en route to New York. He wrote to his wife that he and his traveling companions, his brother, Joaquín and an aide, Juan Togno, had been well received throughout the journey, and that they were entertained frequently.[33]

At the time of González Ortega's departure from Mexico many of the leading republicans had already fled. Others had accepted the Empire and retired to private life. The French temporarily abandoned the southern provinces to Díaz and his forces, but elsewhere in the country the republicans were reduced almost entirely to guerrilla warfare. Early in 1865 Juárez was forced to move his government again, this time to Paso del Norte, where

Bazaine declined to attack him because of the possibility of complications with the United States.

It was under these circumstances, when Juárez alone symbolized the republican government, that the personal struggle between the president and González Ortega finally reached a climax.

González Ortega arrived in New York City early in May, 1865. The Mexican refugees and American friends of Mexico in that city received him as president of the supreme court and gave appropriate entertainments in his honor. It is significant, however, that the Mexican minister in Washington, Matías Romero, discouraged such recognition as much as possible, pointing out that Mexico's cause would be better served by mass rallies than by small private dinners for the president of the supreme court.[34]

On May 22, González Ortega traveled to Washington where Romero received him and welcomed him to his home. While in Washington he was presented to President Johnson and other important political and business figures. Romero reported to Juárez that fortunately González Ortega could not speak English and Johnson did not understand Spanish, so there was no danger that González Ortega would say anything embarassing.[35] González Ortega left Washington on June 1 and returned to New York. He advised Romero that if the news from Mexico was favorable he intended to make plans for an early return there to raise funds and men to fight the French.[36]

The Juárez correspondence during the spring and summer of 1865 indicates that he feared González Ortega and what he might attempt. He constantly reminded his son-in-law, Pedro Santacilia, who was in New York, that González Ortega had no official mission in the United States, and that anything he might hear to the contrary was false. He expressed disappointment over the fact that González Ortega had gone to the United States rather than Sonora or Lower California. He admitted that González Ortega might be planning to return by way of Panama or some other point in the South, but he doubted it. It was more likely,

Juárez felt, that González Ortega simply wanted to rest, and that he would return only to claim the presidency when Juárez' term expired in December.[37]

González Ortega meanwhile requested permission of the Mexican government to raise funds and men in the United States. He reported that his contacts and official position had enabled him to get many promises of aid, but he needed authorization from Juárez. There is no evidence that Juárez answered this request, although he informed Santacilia and Romero that such authorization would not be granted.[38] Rumors continued to circulate concerning González Ortega's plans to return to Mexico and claim the presidency, but they remained only rumors. Juárez was apprehensive of granting him authority to act for the republican government, but it would appear that the administration could have put González Ortega's fame and position to better use.[39]

Whatever González Ortega's intention with reference to his return to Mexico he was delayed by a court action brought against him in New York City. A Colonel William H. Allen alleged that he had represented himself as an agent of the Mexican government and had obtained funds for the aid of Mexico. Allen brought suit to recover these funds when he learned that González Ortega had no official mission. The latter sought the aid of Minister Romero, who obtained a lawyer for him and aided him throughout the trial. Romero informed Juárez that he thought it best to clear González Ortega before the incident caused embarrassment to the Mexican government. The court action, however, kept González Ortega in New York until November 3, 1865, when he was acquitted.[40] There were rumors, but no evidence whatsoever, that the whole case was manufactured by the Juarista elements in order to detain González Ortega in the United States until after the legal expiration of Juárez' term of office.[41]

After the conclusion of the court action brought against him in New York, González Ortega made plans for his return to Mexico. In a conversation with Minister Romero, he insisted that Juárez could not stay in office after the expiration of his term and that if he attempted to do so, González Ortega intended to issue a manifesto objecting to it. At the same time he advised Romero that in such an event he would delay military action until the country called on him. Romero, in reporting this conversation to Juárez, expressed the belief that González Ortega did not intend to cause any real trouble, but that there was considerable danger that other ambitious men might convince him to change his mind.[42]   Thus the stage was set for the final confrontation between Juárez and González Ortega.

NOTES

1. Bancroft, *Mexico,* VI, 73-86, 108.
2. *Ibid.,* 114-115.
3. *Ibid.,* 108-110.
4. Rivera, *Anales,* p. 126. It would appear that González Ortega's appointment was not based upon any real confidence in him by the Juárez administration. In making these arrangements Lerdo traveled quite a bit and conferred with Comonfort, Uraga, and Doblado, but there is no indication that he discussed national problems with González Ortega. Frank A. Knapp, Jr., *The Life of Sebastián Lerdo de Tejada, 1823-1889,* (Austin, 1951), p. 83. The fact that there were others who still respected González Ortega's military ability seems obvious. One example of this is a letter from Placido Vega to Lerdo, Mazatlán, November 1, 1863, in the Plácido Vega Manuscripts (University of California). Once again the writer is indebted to Professor Walter V. Scholes for the use of notes on this collection and others at the University of California.
5. Villaseñor y Villaseñor, *Estudios Históricos,* II, 179, 187. Planchet, *La cuestión,* pp. 209-210, says that this action was taken so as to eliminate González Ortega, but the connection is clear only to Planchet.
6. The members of the commission were Juan Ortiz Careaga and Nicolás Medina, representing Doblado; Martín W. Chávez, representing the governor of Aguascalientes; and Manuel Cabezut, representing González Ortega.
7. Account of the conference in Archivo Juárez Manuscripts. Also included are letters written to Juárez advising him that the commis-

sioners were on their way and urging him to resign. Chávez to Juárez, Zacatecas, January 3, 1864; Doblado to Juárez, Zacatecas, January 3, 1864; and González Ortega to Juárez, Zacatecas, January 4, 1864. On January 20, Juárez wrote to both González Ortega and Doblado advising them of his decision and restating his reasons. General Patoni was approached by González Ortega and Doblado on this matter but he refused to participate. Patoni to Juárez, Durango, January 8, 1864. Undoubtedly others were also approached, but there is no evidence that anyone else actually requested Juárez' resignation.

8. Juárez to Doblado, Saltillo, January 20, 1864 *ibid.* Juárez had reference, to the escape of González Ortega from the French at Orizaba. Even though González Ortega had refused to sign the parole requested by Forey, some of the French felt that he had violated his word in escaping and taking up arms again.

9. González Ortega to Juárez, Zacatecas, January 25, 1864, *ibid.*

10. Zamacois, *Historia de Méjico,* XVII, 99-100, expresses doubt that González Ortega would have made any kind of deal with the French. Zayas Enríquez, *Juárez,* p. 187, generally critical of González Ortega, expresses the belief that he was the victim of a persecution complex and megalomania. It would appear that some persons felt that the action of González Ortega and Doblado was taken in conjunction with Vidaurri, but there is no evidence to back up this assumption. A commission urging Juárez' resignation was sent by Vidaurri a few days after the similar action by González Ortega. Rivera, *Anales,* p. 130. With the confused situation in Mexico at the time it would not be difficult to attach significance to this. Information to the United States certainly considered the commissions related matters. Vice-Consul M. M. Kimmey reported to Major General F. J. Herrán, in Brownsville, Texas, that Vidaurri had made a deal with González Ortega and Doblado under which González Ortega would become president and Vidaurri would become Minister of Foreign Relations. Following this a compromise would be reached with the French. *War of the Rebellion* (Washington, 1891, Series 1), XXXIV, Part II, 223. This information was passed on by Herrán to Brigadier General C. P. Stone on the previous day so other informants must have relayed similar information. *Ibid.,* 232.

11. Juárez, *Archivos privados,* p. 17; González Ortega, *Golpe,* p. 156. Monterrey was considered but doubts about Governor Santiago Vidaurri and rumors of negotiations between him and the French made the city seem inadvisable.

12. González Ortega, *Golpe,* pp. 203-204; Bancroft, *México,* VI, 125.

94

Patoni wrote to Juárez that González Ortega allowed the French to capture Fresnillo with only 50 men. He admitted that all the circumstances should be known before passing judgment. In addition some of the officers under González Ortega were disgusted because an attack was not made on the French. Durango, March 22, 1864, in Archivo Juárez Manuscripts.

13. Juárez to González Ortega, March 15 and 16; Miguel Negrete, Minister of War, to González Ortega, March 16; and Lerdo to González Ortega, March 16, 1864, in González Ortega, *Golpe,* pp. 205-208.

14. Lerdo to González Ortega and Juárez to González Ortega, March 21, 1864, *ibid.,* pp. 208-209.

15. *Ibid.,* p. 209; Bancroft, *Mexico,* VI, 130-131.

16. According to the Convention of Miramar, signed April 10, 1864, it was agreed that the French forces in Mexico should be gradually reduced until they were entirely replaced by Maximilian's Mexican forces. A treasury for the new government was created by a loan from Napoleon. The loan, though unpopular in Mexico, provided funds for the beginning of the empire. Bancroft, *Mexico,* VI, 139-140.

17. *Ibid.,* 132-133.

18. Roeder, *Juárez,* II, 565-567, 570.

19. Rivera, *Anales,* pp. 151-152.

20. Lerdo to González Ortega, September 4 and 5, 1864, in *Colección de leyes, decretos y circulares expedidas por el supremo gobierno de la república, 1863-1867* (México, 1867, 3 vols.), I, 55-58. This will be cited hereafter as *Colección de leyes.*

21. Villaseñor y Villaseñor, *Estudios históricos,* II, 211.

22. Juárez, *Archivos privados,* 30-31.

23. Jesús González Ortega, *The Presidency of México* (New York, 1866), p. 29. See also Galindo y Galindo, *Gran década,* III, 149, and Juan de Dios Arias, *Reseña historia de la formación y operaciones del cuerpo de ejército del norte durante la intervención francesa, sitio de Querétaro y noticias oficiales sobre la captura de Maximiliano, su proceso integro y su muerte* (México, 1867), pp. 2, 190, for further comments on this engagement.

24. Colonel H. M. Day to Major George B. Drake, Brazos Santiago, October 21, 1864, in *War of the Rebellion* (Washington, 1893, Series 1) XLI, Part 1, 888, states that González Ortega was near Camargo with a force ready to take Matamoros, See also *Periódico Oficial,* November 22, 1864.

25. González Ortega to Lerdo, Chihuahua, November 30, 1864, in

Mex. Leg. Corresp., IV, 559-561. See also *Diario Official,* December 3, 1864.

26. Article 80 of the Constitution of 1857. This article and others relative to the question will be found in Zarco, *Historia del congreso,* II, 1007-1013.

27. Lerdo to González Ortega, Chihuahua, November 30, 1864, in *Periódico Oficial,* December 3, 1864.

28. There was certainly reason for doubt on the interpretation of this article since it makes no specific provision for a person holding both federal and state elective offices. Article 118 reads as follows: "ningún individuo puede desempeñar a la vez doz cargos de la Unión de elección popular, pero el nombrado puede elegir entre ambos el que quiera desempeñar." *Ibid.*

29. See above, Chapter V. There is no evidence of the many requests that González Ortega make a choice. It is also interesting to note how many unconstitutional actions could be taken by Juárez because of the emergency, but the same emergency apparently did not warrant González Ortega's holding on to the nominal governship of Zacatecas. Knapp, *Lerdo,* p. 99, states that González Ortega had been brooding over a legal approach to the presidency just prior to this exchange of letters, but there is no real evidence of this. If there were machinations, they may well have been Lerdo's in planning for the eventual extension of Juárez' term as president.

30. González Ortega to his wife, Chihuahua, December 13 and 25, 1864, in González Ortega, *Golpe,* pp. 213-214.

31. González Ortega to Juárez, Chihuahua, December 28, 1864, in *ibid.,* pp. 223-224.

32. Negrete to González Ortega, Chihuahua, December 30, 1864, in *ibid.,* pp. 224-225. The exact wording of this correspondence becomes extremely important at a later date as will be seen. See also Villaseñor y Villaseñor, *Estudios históricos,* II, 231-233.

33. González Ortega to his wife, January 28, February 17 and March 18, 1865, cited in González Ortega, *Golpe,* pp. 214-216. One further reason for this trip to the United States is apparent in these letters. He planned to make arrangements for his wife and son, Laurito, who were then in Zacatecas, to move to the United States to insure their safety and the continuance of his son's education.

34. González Ortega to Juárez, New York, May 9, 1865, in Archivo Juárez Manuscripts; Romero to Minister of Foreign Relations, Washington, April 25, 1865, in *Mex. Leg. Corresp.,* V, 263. A short and relatively impartial account of the following events appears in Ugarte, *Historia de México,* III, 321-323.

35. Romero to Minister of Foreign Relations, Washington, May 27, 1865, in *Mex. Leg. Corresp.,* V, 339-340; Romero to Juárez, Washington, May 25, 1865, in Archivo Juárez Manuscripts. Most of the correspondence between Romero and the Mexican government relative to González Ortega's activities in the United States will also be found in *Correspondencia Ofciial* (sic) *de la legación mexicana en Washington con el Ministerio de Relaciones Exteriores de la república y el Departamento de Estado de Washington sobre la conducta de D. Jesús G. Ortega, 1865-1866* (México, 1869). This will be cited hereafter as *Corresp. conducta.*

36. Romero to Juárez, Washington, June 1, 1865, in Archivo Juárez Manuscripts.

37. Juárez, *Archivos privados,* pp. 52-68.

38. *Ibid.,* p. 79; Romero to Juárez, Washington, June 26, 1865, in González Ortega, *Golpe,* p. 268. See also Juárez to José María de Jesús Carvajal, Chihuahua, June 8, 1865, in Archivo Juárez Manuscripts. González Ortega's request of Juárez to raise troops, New York, May 8, 1865, in *ibid.,* contains Juárez' denial in the margin. As early as May 29, 1865, the interventionist periodical, *Monitor de la Frontera,* reported that González Ortega, Doblado, and Romero were raising an army in the United States to fight under U. S. General Rosencrans. Cited in *Periódico Oficial,* June 17, 1865.

39. Romero to Juárez, Washington, July 14, 1865, in Archivo Juárez Manuscripts and various letters from Juárez to Santacilia in *Archivos privados.*

40. Romero's letters of September 20, October 18, November 2 and 7, 1865, in *Mex. Leg. Corresp.,* V, 642-643, 706, 748-749, 767-768. See Robert Ryal Miller, "Gaspar Sánchez Ochoa: A Mexican Secret Agent in the United States," *The Historian,* XXIII (May, 1961), 323-325, for a more detailed account of the Allen affair.

41. González Ortega, *Golpe,* p. 228.

42. Romero to Minister of Foreign Relations, New York, November 7, 1865, in *Mex. Leg. Corresp.,* V, 767-768.

VII
The Juárez Coup d'Etat

While González Ortega tarried in the United States, a political crisis was brewing in Mexico. Juárez' term was due to expire on December 1, 1865, and under the Constitution of 1857 if, for any reason, an elect⁻n had not been held before the expiration of his term, the president was to step down and the executive power pass to the president of the supreme court. Thus, strict construction of the constitution required that González Ortega become president of the republic on December 1. However, as one historian has pointed out, "It was no time to change horses in midstream,"[1] and Juárez did not intend to relinquish his position as chief executive to González Ortega.

As late as August, 1865, Juárez had not determined the method by which to prorogue his term. What was certain, however, was that González Ortega, as legal successor, was the major obstacle to any Juarista plan to extend the presidential term. Romero held conversations with various persons in the United States to determine the effect any prorogation would have while Juárez began to broach the subject to his friends and other republican leaders in Mexico.[2] Romero seemed to feel that González Ortega would confine himself to written protests against Juárez, but that he would not make any actual military move. Juárez was not so certain. He felt that he could extend his term on the basis of the emergency authority given him by congress, but he also believed that González Ortega or some other republican leader would question the legality of such a move and that this might result in civil war. The president observed, nevertheless, that by the end of November, "circumstances, the law and public opinion" would indicate what road to follow.[3]

Juárez was at least correct in assuming that some important republicans would oppose his attempt to remain in power. Both Prieto, then head of the postal department and editor of the

99

Periódico Oficial, and Manuel Ruiz, who was acting head of the supreme court, had already made their intentions clear, and González Ortega had a number of vocal adherents among the Mexicans in the United States. Some Mexican officers even sent agents to González Ortega, asking him to return to Mexico before November, and promising their support in a declaration against Juárez.[4] There is no evidence that González Ortega accepted any of the offers of military aid and support, although it is likely that he left openings for future acceptance.

An indication of the type of attack which was going to be made on González Ortega appeared in an exchange of letters between Juárez and Prieto in October, 1865. Prieto asked to be relieved of his duties with the post office, and in replying that this was impossible, Juárez reminded Prieto that "I never have said to you nor authorized you to say to General González Ortega in my name, that he could remain indefinitely away from his country."[5] Prieto then wrote to Juárez saying that he had never intimated to González Ortega that indefinite residence in the United States was authorized, but he had understood from Juárez that it was permissible for him to work in conjunction with Romero. Prieto had thus assumed that the president was not averse to González Ortega's remaining away from Mexico.[6] Juárez immediately denied this assumption, stating that he had written to González Ortega on September 7, 1865, refusing him the authority he had requested.[7] Another exchange of letters followed, with Prieto refusing to believe Juárez, and the latter reasserting that he had simply offered to answer González Ortega in a courteous and polite manner, nothing more. Prieto's resignation was also accepted for presentation to the proper authorities.[8]

Juárez' next step, which foreshadowed González Ortega's final disagreement, took place on October 28, 1865. On that date Minister of Relations Sebastián Lerdo de Tejada issued a circular to the various state governors giving instructions concerning the treatment of generals, chiefs, and officials who had absented themselves from Mexico. According to this circular such men were to be imprisoned and held for trial by the first military or political authority having the opportunity. This order affected not only those Mexicans who had departed from the country without authority, but also those who, after obtaining permission to leave the country, had remained away for more than four months.[9] Juárez undoubtedly intended that this order include González Ortega, but it is doubtful that many of the state governors would have taken action against the president of the supreme court.[10]

On November 8, 1865, Juárez took the final steps necessary to his continuance in office by issuing two decrees. The first extended the functions of the president and the president of the supreme court until it became possible to elect new officers. Juárez claimed authority for this decree because of extraordinary faculties granted to him by congress and also on the basis of the Constitution of 1857, which provided only for the temporary succession to the presidency and not for extreme emergencies such as the war then going on.[11] The second decree declared that González Ortega had voluntarily abandoned the post as president of the supreme court when he remained in a foreign country without permission of or commission by the government. In addition González Ortega was to be arrested and tried on his reappearance in Mexico for the crime of desertion of his post as a general of the army. This action would be taken under Article 104 of the constitution. To provide for the possible lack of a successor to the presidency it was further decreed that Juárez would name a substitute president of the supreme court.[12]

The issuance of these brought immediate protests from some of the republican leaders still in Mexico. The American consul in Mexico observed that many persons considered the decrees as unjust and illegal, but that no violent opposition was likely unless or until González Ortega appeared on the frontier.[13]

González Ortega was not immediately aware of the steps which had been taken against him, and he was more concerned at the time with obtaining funds to finance his return to Mexico. He requested money from Romero for this purpose, but was refused and forced to turn elsewhere.[14] Romero did, however, obtain the necessary permission from the United States Army for his passage to Mexico.[15] After González Ortega's departure from New York late in November, Romero was compelled to pay the debts which had been contracted during the court action with Allen. González Ortega had promised to pay the lawyers, and consul-general Juan N. Navarro, who served as interpreter, had backed up his promise. As a result Romero felt that the debt should be paid to avoid any embarrassment to the Mexican government.[16]

While González Ortega was en route to Mexico, Juárez evidently still felt some doubt as to the extension of his own term of office. When González Ortega failed to appear by December 1 he wrote to his son-in-law that here was evidence which justified his action. If he had not moved when he did, Juárez explained, the country would have been left without a legal head on December 1, and anarchy would have followed. Juárez expressed the belief that he had saved Mexico, and he was, therefore, content.[17]

González Ortega reached the southern part of the United States before learning of the November 8 decrees. He issued a protest against these decrees from Eagle Pass, Texas, on December 21, 1865. In this brief protest González Ortega asserted that Juárez' actions were unconstitutional, dictatorial, and insulting to the Mexican people. He added that the attacks on his personal and official character were unfounded and unwarranted.[18]

This protest was followed on December 26 by a lengthy manifesto issued from San Antonio, Texas, which detailed the events leading up to Juárez' "illegal usurpation". González Ortega began this protest with the assertation that he had acted, and would continue to act, for the good of his country and not merely for himself. Juárez' illegal actions must be restricted, and, as the legal successor to the presidency, González Ortega believed it to be his duty to make the protest. He quoted the article of the constitution which set the length of the president's term and provided for the succession of the president of the supreme court in the event the office were left vacant "from any cause."[19] This particular phrase would indicate that Juárez did not have the legal right to extend his term even in view of the war. In addition González Ortega argued that under Article 95 of the constitution a magistrate might resign his office only for a grave reason, and this renunciation must be approved by congress or the permanent deputation of that body. Under his interpretation González Ortega demonstrated that he could not have given up the post of president of the supreme court when he assumed the governorship of Zacatecas in 1863.[20]

González Ortega also brought up Title IV of the constitution, which concerned the responsibilities of public functionaries. Under this section congress, acting as a grand jury, was to decide whether there was cause for proceeding against the president of the court when he was accused of a crime of the common order, such as the charge of desertion brought against González Ortega in the second decree of November 8. González Ortega could thus maintain that under the constitution Juárez had no authority to order his arrest and trial. The congressional decrees granting Juárez extraordinary powers specifically stated that the executive had no authority to contravene Title IV of the constitution in any way.

The protest continued by pointing out that beginning in 1861 González Ortega had served as constitutional governor of Zacatecas and at various times after his assumption of that post he had been elected interim president of the court and acted as governor and military commander of San Luis Potosí and military commander of Aguascalientes and Tamaulipas. During this time there had been no objection to the duplication of offices. Following his election as constitutional president of the supreme court, an office which he had gained in spite of the opposition of the administration, González Ortega served as a general of the army and governor and military commander of Puebla. This was possible and permissible in view of the urgent military needs of the country, and because it was impossible for the court to function in such critical times.

As to his prolonged stay in the United States, González Ortega published the letter already mentioned granting him permission to leave his post for an indefinite time with the understanding that he would continue the war by entering Mexico at some other point. Although he had remained in a foreign land, he asserted that Juárez had been fully informed of his movements. He declared that he had received no reply to his request for authority to enroll volunteers and otherwise secure resources for the republican armies, and that a private lawsuit had been concocted to detain him as long as possible.

González Ortega also described previous attempts by the Juárez faction to obtain his removal from the post of chief justice for having acted as governor of Zacatecas, and he accused Juárez of attempting to injure his prestige as a military leader by placing him in critical positions with insufficient forces. All of this had been done, González Ortega implied, for the purpose of removing him from the political scene before the expiration of Juárez' legal term, and the safety of Mexico had been endangered simply because Juárez wished to remain in power. The decrees issued on November 8 were not only illegal but founded upon false and incomplete facts — the culmination of a long-planned coup d'etat. What González Ortega was saying was that Juárez' term had expired and that he, González Ortega, was now president of Mexico.

González Ortega was not alone in opposing the extension of Juárez' term of office. Manuel Ruiz, now acting head of the supreme court, protested on constitutional grounds in hopes of advancing his own claim to the presidency. General Epitacio Huerta, whose arrest Juárez had ordered, was also interested in eliminating Juárez so that he could return safely to Mexico.[21] Other less important figures undoubtedly found themselves in a similar predicament, and they saw the removal of Juárez as a partial solution to their problems. Others objected to Juárez' actions because they honestly felt that the constitution had been violated.[22] Guillermo Prieto was González Ortega's only supporter who took an active part in the conflict. He poured out letters to his friends and acquaintances advancing arguments in González Ortega's behalf, and made clear his fear and suspicion of both Juárez and his chief advisor, Lerdo.[23]

During the weeks following González Ortega's protest from San Antonio, Juárez appeared apprehensive of some precipitate action by González Ortega or his followers.[24] He wrote to Santacilia, however, that nothing could happen since González Ortega lacked the necessary elements for a military move. Juárez also expressed surprise over the fact that some Mexicans who did not desire González Ortega for president still did not approve of the November decree accusing González Ortega of crimes against the state.[25]

Lerdo, who must have had an opportunity to test his logic on the soul-searching Juárez, wrote Romero in January, 1866, advancing some of the reasons for the issuance of the second decree of November 8, so that Romero would have an official explanation to pass on to the United States government. In this letter Lerdo reviewed González Ortega's conduct after the defeat at Puebla and again asserted that he had abandoned the presidency of the court. Lerdo repeated the attack on González Ortega's actions at the battle of Majoma, and stated that the government refrained from acting against him at that time only because of the critical situation which existed. Once the general left the country and failed to return, however, the government was compelled to act.[26]

Lerdo might also have pointed out that conditions in Mexico were no longer as critical as they had been at the time of the battle of Majoma. The collapse of Maximilian's empire was imminent. The end of the American Civil War, complications in Europe and disappointment with both Maximilian and Mexico had cooled Napoleon's ardor for the enterprise. Bazaine was ordered to withdraw from Mexico, in spite of Maximilian's protests, and the slow retreat began in March, 1866. As a ring of republican armies began to form and prepare for an advance on Mexico City, Maximilian resolved to retain his throne without French aid. The return of Miramón and Márquez from Europe, ready to fight for the cause of religion and privilege, improved the outlook for his army, for both were experienced generals. By summer, however, the empire consisted of little more than the cities of Mexico, Puebla, Querétaro, and Veracruz.[27]

Juárez could thus afford to be patient and fairly complacent, for the empire was practically a thing of the past, at least insofar as French support was concerned. At the same time the majority of the republicans accepted the extension of his presidential term. When Juárez received González Ortega's protest and manifesto issued in December, 1865, he wrote to Santacilia: "I shall answer it as it should be answered, but of course a decorous answer, for it is repugnant to the dignity of a government to descend to the forbidden ground on which the silly criminal González Ortega basks." Despite the above-mentioned protests Juárez was also able to report that his government was being obeyed and respected without question by the authorities and the people.[28]

Although Juárez was willing publicly to ignore González Ortega as much as possible in the months following the coup d'etat, the constant danger that González Ortega might return preoccupied him. González Ortega, meanwhile, was not content to let Juárez remain in power so easily, and he began to take steps to oust him from office. There is little doubt that both men were motivated in part by personal ambition, but Juárez apparently acted also upon the belief that practical considerations for the safety of Mexico rather than theoretical and sometimes vague constitutional interpretations should govern. He was to be right only because he was to win.

NOTES

1. Roeder, *Juárez*, II, 613.
2. Juárez, *Archivos privados*, pp. 85, 90-91.
3. Romero to Minister of Foreign Relations, New York, August 19, 1865, in *Mex. Leg. Corresp.*, V, 572-573. It is possible that Romero contributed to the pressure on Juárez by submitting his resignation on September 4, giving as his reason the possibility that González Ortega might become president. *Ibid.*, 605. Nothing indicates that Romero was given some assurances even at this date. Juárez, *Archivos privados*, pp. 90-91.
4. Romero to Minister of Foreign Relations, New York, September 23, 1865, in *Mex. Leg. Corresp.*, V, 651.
5. Prieto to Juárez and reply, Paso del Norte, October 1, 1865, in Archivo Juárez Manuscripts.
6. *Ibid.*
7. This letter which Juárez claims to have written does not appear in any of the correspondence of the persons involved. Although Juárez' intention to answer in this manner is evident, there is no positive proof that he actually communicated his opinion to González Ortega.
8. October 2, 1865, in Archivo Juárez Manuscripts.
9. D y L, *Legislación*, IX, 717-718.
10. Juárez, *Archivos privados*, p. 100; Villaseñor y Villaseñor, *Estudios históricos*, II, 240-243. See above Chapter VI.
11. D y L, *Legislación*, IX, 718-719, and *Periódico Oficial*, November 9, 1865, contain the text of the decree. The special powers mentioned were granted by a series of decrees by Congress beginning in December, 1861. The chief executive was to take any steps necessary to save the independence of Mexico, the constitutional form of government, and the principles of the laws of reform. These decrees will be found in *ibid.*, as follows: December 11, 1861, 334; May 3, 1862, 440; October 27, 1862, 548-549; May 27, 1863, 622.
12. D y L, *Legislación*, IX, 719-721. Knapp, *Lerdo*, pp. 101-104, credits Lerdo with the authorship of these decrees and assumes that he at least collaborated with Juárez in determining the course of action to be followed. More definite in the assertion that Lerdo influenced Juárez to extend his term is Manuel Ruiz, *Exposición que el C. Lic. Manuel Ruiz, ministro constitucional de la suprema corte de justicia de la nación, presenta al soberano congreso de la unión* (México, 1868).
13. Reuben W. Creel to Seward, Chihuahua, November 22, 1865, in

U. S. House Executive Documents, 39 Cong., 1 Sess., (1865-1866), No. 73, Part 2, 523.

14. González Ortega to Romero and reply, New York, November 12, 1865, in *Mex. Leg. Corresp.,* V, 777-780.
15. General U. S. Grant to officials of the United States, Washington, November 10, 1865, in *ibid.,* 780.
16. Romero to Minister of Foreign Relations, Washington, November 23, 1865, in *ibid.,* 318.
17. Juárez, *Archivos privados,* pp. 105, 107-108.
18. This protest appears in several places, including *Corresp. conducta,* pp. 33-35; González Ortega, *Presidency of Mexico,* pp. 9-10; and *Mex. Leg. Corresp.,* VIII, 463. Villaseñor y Villaseñor, *Estudios históricos,* II, 319, expresses the belief that this protest was not written by González Ortega. Probably González Ortega did have advice in composing the protest, but there is no reason to assume that he could not have written it himself.
19. Article 82 of the Constitution of 1857.
20. This manifesto, dated San Antonio de Béjar, December 26, 1865, will be found in *Mex. Leg. Corresp.,* VIII, 464-489, and *Corresp. conducta,* pp. 35-90.
21. Villaseñor y Villaseñor, *Estudios históricos,* II, 298-304; Rivera, *Anales,* p. 177.
22. Among those who were listed among González Ortega's supporters in the United States were Felipe B. Berriozábal, Santiago Vicario, Epitacio Huerta, Gaspar Sánchez Ochoa, Pablo Rocha y Portu, Eulalio Degollado, Francisco Paz, José Montesinos, Miguel Negrete, Jesús Fuentes Muñez, Francisco Ibarra Ramos — all military men — and the lawyers, Juan José Baz, Cipriano Robert, and Rafael de Zayas, Villaseñor y Villaseñor, *Estudios históricos,* II, 321.
23. *Ibid.,* 322.
24. Numerous letters from Juárez to Santacilia in January and February, 1866, in *Archivos privados.*
25. *Ibid.,* pp 121-123.
26. Lerdo to Romero, El Paso, January 27, 1866, in *Mex. Leg. Corresp.,* VI, 465-468. Villaseñor y Villaseñor, *Estudios históricos,* I, 78, states that, ignoring all else, Juárez declared González Ortega could not be president for having abandoned national territory, the same thing he, himself, had done in 1858. See *ibid.,* II, 245-273, for a criticism of the November 8 decrees.
27. Bancroft, *Mexico,* VI, 207-259; Roeder, *Juárez,* II, 616-644.
28. Juárez, *Archivos privados,* p. 125.

VIII
Protest and Imprisonment

While Juárez worked to solidify his regime, González Ortega continued to protest the coup d'etat. On February 3, 1866, while still in San Antonio, he addressed a circular to various Mexicans asking for their opinions with regard to Juárez' actions.[1] Armed with the most favorable replies to this request, he returned to New York where, with the aid of Joaquín Villalobos, he prepared a publication in Spanish,[2] incorporating his previous protests and the letters received in reply to his circular.[3] The letters from Patoni and Huerta indicated that they were disposed to aid him against Juárez.[4] Prieto replied by sending copies of the communications he had exchanged with Juárez in October.[5] Prieto also included a letter in which he stated that he hated the Juárez decrees, and that they were certainly directed against González Ortega. Prieto added that he pleaded not for González Ortega as an individual, but as the personification of the right. As proof of the injustice of the decrees, Prieto pointed out that González Ortega had left Mexico on leave of absence, had advised the government of his residence, placed his services at its disposal, had written directly to Juárez, and still had not received any sign of the government's disapproval.[6] The remaining letters included in the publication were from men of little influence in Mexican politics.[7]

It was evidently González Ortega's plan to issue his publication and then invade Mexico with troops raised in the United States, hoping that once the forces of the empire were defeated any support for Juárez would be seriously weakened.[8] When the French intervention ended various factions would struggle for power, and he felt that the moderate element would take over under Lerdo's leadership.[9] Thus González Ortega believed that his own return was necessary not only to maintain constitutional government in Mexico, but also to prevent the destruction of the

Liberal party and its program by Juárez and Lerdo. As he wrote Plácido Vega, he was trying to save Mexico's honor by showing that Juárez' actions were his alone and not those of the Liberal party or the nation.[10] But González Ortega's return to Mexico was not as swift nor as successful as he seemed to have expected.

Upon the appearance of González Ortega's published protest, Minister Romero suggested to the Juárez administration that it might be well to issue a reply to counteract any bad effect his documents may have caused.[11] Juárez agreed, and in New York Pantaleon Tovar began to prepare a reply.[12] This pamphlet incorporated various answers to González Ortega's circular which the Zacatecan had not seen fit to publish. In addition, other correspondence favorable to Juárez was included.[13]

The replies to González Ortega published by the administration were not favorable to Juárez in every case, but they were unanimous in that all of them deplored the possibility of armed opposition to the president and placed the immediate task of expelling the French above any constitutional question. Typical of the reluctance of the correspondents to express themselves is this statement by Juan J. Baz, a former member of the Mexican congress: "As a private Mexican citizen, who is not a judge of his country to decide the acts of his government, I agree with you [that no opposing banners should be raised while Mexican independence is being defended], and will do my best to support that government. As there would be no use in the future expression of my opinion, you will pardon me for not answering more particularly.[14] Francisco Zarco expressed the same sentiment in the following words: "As to my approval or disapproval here of acts of the government of Mexico, representing our nationality, I would be failing in my duty if I excited controversies that could only serve to strengthen the foreign usurpers."[15]Cipriano Robert was more positive in his support of Juárez than most of the others in that he asserted his belief that the executive had acted in accordance with powers conferred upon him by congress. Pantaleón Tovar, not surprisingly, expressed a similar belief that Juárez had acted in accordance with the constitution.[16] The remaining letters were from Gregorio Méndez, governor of Tabasco, and Alejandro García, second-in-command to Porfirio Díaz, both of whom announced their support of Juárez and his decrees.[17]

An exchange of letters between Villalobos and Green Clay Smith, United States Congressman from Kentucky, completed the publication.[18] Smith, who was working closely with Romero, had introduced a resolution in the House of Representatives requesting the Secretary of State to submit all the available information on the expiration of Juárez' term. Villalobos took advantage of this apparent opportunity to spread propaganda and wrote to Smith advising him that González Ortega would soon publish all the documents on the subject.[19]

On April 30, 1866, Lerdo issued a circular which served as an official reply to the protest and manifesto published by González Ortega in December of the previous year. After defending the extension of Juárez' term of office, Lerdo asserted that González Ortega remained outside of Mexico without permission of the government, and that on September 7, 1865, Juárez had refused to grant him a commission from the government. Lerdo defended the order to arrest González Ortega on the grounds that it would be absurd to suppose that congress should not punish public functionaries during the war. As to the question of holding two elective offices, Lerdo had this to say: "By article 118 of the constitution, no man can hold two elective offices at the same time, but must say which he will fill; this I stated in the decree. I also said, that though federal offices were meant, the article applied to state offices too." Lerdo also pointed out that the other offices which González Ortega held while he was governor of Zacatecas were appointive, not elective.[20]

Most of the circular consisted of a detailed denial of the various charges which González Ortega had leveled at the government. Lerdo concluded with the statement that González Ortega had not explained why, in time of war, he had deserted his country and taken up residence in a foreign land, nor had he proved the unconstitutionality of the November 8 decrees. The attack on González Ortega was continued on June 5, 1866, in a brief article in the official periodical. It reviewed the answers González Ortega had received to his circular in February, and then attempted to discredit those persons who had written favorable replies.[21]

Perhaps the most impressive publication by the government in defense of the prorogation of Juárez' term appeared in the United States on June 30, 1866. It was in reply to an English translation of the pamphlet González Ortega had published in March.[22] (The pamphlet reviewed arguments and included a new discussion of the constitutional question involved.[23]) It was agreed that Article 82 of the constitution, if taken alone and strictly interpreted, would give the presidency temporarily to González Ortega as chief justice. Taken in conjunction with articles which precede it, however, and in view of the "well-known intent of its framers," it would have been a direct violation of the spirit of the articles to allow the substitute president to become the permanent president. According to the spirit of the law, Juárez was thus within his legal rights when he prolonged his term of office, and even more than that, the Mexican people preferred Juárez' decision.[24] An appendix to this publication contained letters or extracts of letters from every state governor in Mexico. Every one of them expressed approval of the president's course, and asserted that the people living in their jurisdictions likewise approved.[25]

This exchange of charges in English was motivated by González Ortega's desire to convince the United States to recognize his claim to the presidency. Juárez, on the other hand, was desirous of retaining that recognition for his own administration. In July, 1866, González Ortega visited Secretary of State Seward and pressed his claim.[26] Although there is no indication that the United States ever seriously considered recognizing González Ortega as president of Mexico, especially when the majority of the Mexican people continued to accept Juárez, González Ortega wrote to Miguel Negrete in June, 1866, that Juárez was no longer recognized in the United States and a loan was in the process of being arranged with him as legitimate president.[27] This news must have been circulated by González Ortega as encouragement to his followers since there was actually no reason for him to believe it.

During the summer of 1866 activities in favor of González Ortega increased with his plans for returning to Mexico. Sánchez Ochoa began to issue publications in the United States asking for recognition of González Ortega as president while Marcelino Canero initiated an unsuccessful move to proclaim in favor of González Ortega in the state of Coahuila. Canero was shot when the movement failed.[28] González Ortega advised Negrete that he did not anticipate any opposition to his return, but that should any arise, he would meet it with an armed force of American volunteers.[29]

Prieto apparently continued to be the most prolific letter-writer in support of González Ortega. He wrote to numerous persons inviting their support of his cause, in addition to carrying on much correspondence at González Ortega's request.[30] It is obvious, however, that Prieto was not convinced that the Zacatecan would make a good president. He simply opposed Juárez for his usurpation of power. On one occasion he wrote to a friend that it was not a question of personalities, and if "Juárez and Ortega were contrasted, they would both lose."[31]

There were various persons in the United States who encouraged González Ortega in his opposition to Juárez, usually in the hope of personal profit. The name of John C. Fremont appears from time to time in various connections as González Ortega's leading American supporter.[32] Another American, William H. McKee, obtained a contract from González Ortega for establishing a mint in San Francisco. For this privilege McKee was to pay González Ortega $60,000. Within a month, however, McKee had written to Juárez' minister of the treasury, J. M. Iglesias, asking for a similar contract with the Juárez administration, since he had neither the wish nor the expectation that González Ortega would succeed in his fight against Juárez.[33]

Still another side to the Juárez-González Ortega struggle developed out of the French decision to withdraw from Mexico. As early as March, 1866, an envoy from Maximilian's military cabinet was authorized to journey from Mexico City to Zacatecas on a confidential mission having to do with González Ortega. The pecuniary interests of France, which had become the imperial government's primary consideration, demanded a firm regime in Mexico, and the attitude of the United States and the strength of the Liberals left little hope for the formation of a Conservative government. The only hope for the French in obtaining a government favorable to their interests, therefore, was to set up a prominent Liberal leader in opposition to Juárez. Among the possibilities were González Ortega, Díaz, Ruiz, and Lerdo.[34] Of the possible choices, Napoleon and others felt that González Ortega offered the best possibilities. In addition to his avowed supporters there were some good Liberal chiefs who objected to the Juárez coup d'etat, but because of the French invasion they had refused to break with his government. There was the possibility, furthermore, that a large number of those Mexicans who had accepted the intervention would support González Ortega if they were convinced that he would be more lenient with them than Juárez. There was, consequently, considerable speculation over the possibility of establishing González Ortega in power, and also rumors with regard to agreements between him and the French.[35]

There is no reason to assume, however, that any agreement with the French was ever offered González Ortega. In October, 1866, Napoleon's aide-de-camp, Eduard de Castelnau, was sent to Mexico to take over direction of the political movements. Castelnau, who had been instructed to approach González Ortega, very soon expressed his disapproval of this plan. He discarded González Ortega with these words: "Not well regarded in the eyes of all parties because of his political ineptitude and his immorality, he is, apparently, a prostitute of low grade, a Lovelace of the sidewalks, a man lost in vices and lacking all the qualities required by the part proposed for him."[36]

In the autumn of 1866 González Ortega finally made definite plans for his return to Mexico. Arriving in New Orleans in October, he published a manifesto in various newspapers announcing his intention to return to his country as president.

On October 25, Major General P. H. Sheridan, the American commander in New Orleans, dispatched an order to the commander at Brazos de Santiago, Texas, informing him of González Ortega's plans and instructing him to arrest González Ortega on his arrival and hold him until he received further orders.[37] González Ortega protested against Sheridan's action, insisting that the United States had no right to intervene,[38] and on October 29 he preceeded with his plans by embarking with several companions for Brazos de Santiago.

On November 3, 1866, González Ortega and his companions landed at Brazos de Santiago and were immediately arrested by an American officer, Burton Drew, who in turn transferred them to Captain John Paulson for detention if they did not desire to return to New Orleans by the same ship on which they had arrived.[39] González Ortega chose not to return and was detained at Brazos de Santiago for more than a month. On November 5 he addressed a lengthy protest to Captain Paulson who transmitted the letter through the various military channels until it finally reached Seward on December 8, two days after the military authorities had released him.[40] In the interim González Ortega had issued two other written protests and several oral complaints.[41]

While González Ortega was thus confined, other actions by the United States either intentionally or unintentionally thwarted his efforts to oppose the Juárez government effectively. The state of Matamoros on the Mexican-United States border was under the control of Servando Canales, who had proclaimed in favor of González Ortega, and it was to this state that González Ortega evidently planned to go. Another Liberal chief, Santiago Tapia, marched against Canales in November, both as a supporter of Juárez and as a long-time personal enemy of Canales.[42] Thomas D. Sedgwick, the American commander at Brownsville, Texas, led U. S. troops into Mexico and occupied the town of Matamoros. The alleged object of the occupation was to protect American citizens, but in effect it transferred the city to the Juaristas.[43] On November 30 Sedgwick withdrew from Mexico and was relieved of his command. The Juárez government protested this intervention by American troops in spite of the supposed collusion between the American commander and General Mariano Escobedo, who had replaced Tapia as head of the Juaristas in Matamoros.[44] Although there was no official connection between this movement of American forces into Mexico and the detention of González Ortega in the United States, it is nevertheless true that Sheridan notified Grant on December 11 that, with Canales out of the way, he had been able to release González Ortega upon Escobedo's promise to look after him.[45]

Following his release on December 6, González Ortega went to Brownsville, where he remained until December 26, at which time he entered Mexico. On the date of his entry González Ortega issued a new manifesto directed against Juárez which recounted the previous charges and added a new one against Romero for not defending Mexico more vigorously in the face of American intervention. Romero and by implication Juárez, were accused of compromising Mexican honor for their personal interests. The document concluded with strong intimations of leniency toward collaborators and imperialists.[46]

González Ortega, accompanied by Patoni, finally arrived in Zacatecas, where on January 8 he announced himself to Governor Miguel Auza, a Juárez appointee. Auza evidently attempted to persuade González Ortega to leave Zacatecas so that he would not have to carry out the arrest order, but González Ortega insisted upon a conference. At the meeting he urged his claim to the presidency on Auza; but the latter, after refusing to acknowledge the claim, ordered González Ortega and Patoni arrested.

The two prisoners were immediately transferred to Saltillo where they remained for two months.[47]

The French, meanwhile, were evacuating Mexico rapidly, but Maximilian was still determined not to abdicate. General Bazine made one last effort to force Maximilian's departure by destoying all the cannon and ammunition which he could not take with him, but when this failed the last of the French troops marched out of Mexico City on February 5, 1867. They began embarking at Veracruz on February 14, and a month later Bazaine left Mexico. The republicans' advance was uncontested until Juárez reached Zacatecas, when Miramón penetrated to the capital of the state and almost succeeded in capturing Juárez. Retreating from the town, however, Miramón was attacked and routed at San Joaquín on February 6 by the advancing republican forces. From this point he retreated to Querétaro, where Maximilian, who had taken the field as supreme commander of his armies, had established a front to protect the capital. Invested by about forty thousand republican soldiers under the command of Escobedo, Querétaro held out for almost a hundred days, from February 19 until May 15. A last-minute plan of escape was foiled by the treachery of one of Maximilian's Mexican officers, and the emperor was captured with his entire staff. He and his leading lieutenants, Miramón and Mejía, were held for trial by a military court.

In spite of the opposition and protests of various foreign powers, the emperor and his two companions were put on trial on June 11 and sentenced to death on the 15th. On June 19 the three men fell before a firing squad on the Hill of Bells near Querétaro.[48] A brief campaign against Márquez, who attempted a desperate defense of Mexico City, ended on June 21 when General Díaz entered the capital. On July 15 Juárez, accompanied by members of his cabinet, made a triumphal entry into the city. The war and the empire were at an end.[49]

In spite of this victory Juárez was not in an enviable position. The transition from war to peace brought new troubles and sources of conflict. One month after his return the president took steps to end his irregular tenure in power. He called for general elections and announced a series of constitutional reforms to be submitted to popular referendum.[50] The reforms were opposed in part out of a fear of increased power for the president and in part because of the method by which they were to be effected. Juárez was accused of trying to encroach on the powers of the legislature, and protests by the press and various political groups increased the general uneasiness.[51]

These differences led to the organization of an opposition party which settled upon Porfirio Díaz as its candidate for the presidency. When the elections were held in October, nevertheless, no one, including the opposition, was particularly surprised when Juárez was elected. Sebastián Lerdo de Tejada, also in competition with Díaz, was elected president of the supreme court.[52] On December 19 congress declared Juárez president-elect, and on December 25 he assumed the duties for the term to end on November 30, 1871.[53] The proposed constitutional reforms were temporarily forgotten.

The election of Juárez and Lerdo dealt the final blow to any hopes which González Ortega may have had for general recognition by the Mexican people. He was still capable of issuing protests against the administration, but his major role henceforth was to be that of a figurehead, willingly or unwillingly, for the opponents of Juárez. His arbitrary imprisonment and his personal quarrel with the president were still to supply considerably fuel for the opposition press, but the honest supporters of his claims were few in number and becoming increasingly difficult to find.[54]

NOTES

1. González Ortega to Juan José Baz, San Antonio, February 3, 1866, in Archivo Juárez Manuscripts. See also *Mex. Leg. Corresp.*, VIII, 489-492.

2. Santacilia to Juárez, New York, March 1, 1866, in Archivo Juárez

Manuscripts.
3. This publication was later translated into English with the title, *The Presidency of Mexico.* This work will be cited hereinafter as *Protest.*
4. Patoni to González Ortega, San Antonio, February 4, 1866; Patoni to Juárez, San Antonio, December 15, 1865; Huerta to González Ortega, New York, February 26, 1866, in *Protest,* pp. 63-68, and *Mex. Leg. Corresp.,* VIII, 493-497.
5. Various letters between Prieto and Juárez, San Antonio, October 1 and 2, 1865; González Ortega to Prieto, San Antonio, February 3, 1866, and reply, February 15, 1866, in *Protest,* pp. 68-70, and *Mex. Leg. Corresp.,* VIII, 497-502. See above Chapter VII.
6. Prieto to Pancho, Paso del Norte, October 31, 1865, in *Protest,* pp. 70-75, and *Mex. Leg. Corresp.,* VIII, 498-500.
7. Fernando Poucel to González Ortega, San Antonio, February 6, 1866; Manuel Quesada to González Ortega, San Antonio, December 18, 1865; Joaquín Villalobos to González Ortega, New York, October 7, 1865, and February 22, 1866; Francisco Ibarra to González Ortega, February 25, 1866; and Juan Togno, J. Rivera, and Juan N. Enríquez Orestes to González Ortega, February 20, 1866, in *Protest,* pp. 79-88, and *Mex. Leg. Corresp.,* VIII, 502-505.
8. Telegrams from González Ortega to Vega, New York, March 27 and 28, 1866, in Vega Manuscripts. González Ortega expected considerable support from Vega, Patoni, Berriozábal, and Huerta.
9. González Ortega to Vega, New York, March 30, 1866, in *ibid.*
10. González Ortega to Vega, New York, March 20, 1866, in *ibid.*
11. Romero to Minister of Foreign Relations, Washington, March 24, 1866, in *Circulares y otras publicaciones hechas por la legación mexicana en Washington durante la guerra de intervención, 1862-1867* (México, 1868, 2 vols.), I, 105-106. This will be cited here-inafter as *Circulares legación.*
12. Romero to Minister of Foreign Relations, Washington, March 24, 1866, in *ibid,* I, 106.
13. *Ibid,* 108-134. See also *U. S. House Executive Documents,* 39 Cong., 2 Sess., (1866-1867), No. 17, 126-134. This defense also appears in *Corresp. conducta,* pp. 91-135, and *Mex. Leg. Corresp.,* VII, 228-231.
14. Baz to González Ortega, New York, February 23, 1866, in Archivo Juárez Manuscripts.
15. Zarco to González Ortega, New York, February 24, 1866, in *Circulares legación,* I, 122-127. Both Leandro Cuevas and Berriozábal answered in much the same terms. Berriozábal did state that he did not entirely approve of the decrees, but that González Ortega's

patriotism should force him to accept them. Cuevas to González Ortega, no place, February 23, 1866, and Berriozábal to González Ortega, New York, February 23, 1866, in *ibid.*, 117-122.

16. Robert to González Ortega, New York, February 27, 1866, and Tovar to González Ortega, New York, February 28, 1866, in *ibid.*, 128-131.

17. Méndez to Juárez, February 2, 1866, and García to Juárez, February 26, 1866, in *ibid.*, 117 and 127.

18. Villalobos to Smith, New York, February 28, 1866, and reply, March 2, 1866, in *ibid.*, 131-133.

19. Romero to Minister of Foreign Relations, Washington, March 8, 1866, in *ibid.*, 103-104. See also Romero to Juárez, Washington, March 3, 1866, in González Ortega, *Golpe*, pp. 315-316.

20. Circular of the Minister of Foreign Relations, Paso del Norte, April 30, 1866, in *Mex. Leg. Corresp.*, VI, 636-658, and in *Colección de leyes*, pp. 9-53.

21. Cited in *Mex. Leg. Corresp.*, VIII, 516-517.

22. This translation, published early in June, was being circulated among the American senators and representatives in Washington. Romero to Minister of Foreign Relations, Washington, June 24, 1866, in *Corresp. conducta*, pp. 152-153.

23. This reply was written and put together by a Robert Dale Owen in Washington from information supplied by Romero. Romero reported to Juárez that it would be circulated among the American congressmen as soon as possible. *Ibid.*, pp. 156-157; Romero to Juárez, Washington, June 20, 1866, in González Ortega, *Golpe*, p. 324.

24. *Mex. Leg. Corresp.*, VIII, 508-515; *Corresp. conducts*, pp. 157-168.

25. Letters from the following were included: Porfirio Díaz, governor of Oaxaca; Alejandro García, governor of Veracruz; Mariano Escobedo, governor of Nuevo León; A. S. Viesca, governor of Coahuila; Domingo Rubi, governor of Sinaloa; J. García Morales, governor of Sonora; José M. J. Carvajal, governor of Tamaulipas; Nicolás de Regules, governor of Michoacán; G. Méndez, governor of Tabasco; José A. Godoy, governor of Chiapas; Diego Álvarez, governor of Guerrero; General Ramón Corona, commander of the forces of Sinaloa and Jalisco; and Juan Álvarez, commander-in-chief of the southern military district.

26. Romero to Juárez, Washington, July 7, 1866, in Archivo Juárez Manuscripts.

27. González Ortega to Negrete, New York, June 25, 1866, in *ibid.*

28. Prieto to Negrete, San Antonio, May 11, 1866, and Romero to

Minister of Foreign Relations, Washington, July 1, 1866, in *Mex. Leg. Çorresp.*, VIII, 1 and 519; Juárez, *Archivos privados*, p. 160.

29. González Ortega to Negrete, New York, June 25, 1866, in Archivo Juárez Manuscripts; Prieto to Juan Mateos, San Antonio, May 11, 1866, in *Diario Imperio*, July 20, 1866. Negrete was probably as active as anyone in support of González Ortega, Knapp, *Lerdo,* p. 101 points out that Negrete, a former and discredited Minister of War, and Prieto were personal enemies of Lerdo as well as opponents of Juárez' actions. Negrete sent out a circular from Bravo on January 27, 1866, to a number of Mexican leaders asking them to join González Ortega (Archivo Juárez Manuscripts). Most of the recipients apparently refused. Francisco Naranjo to Negrete, Valladama, February 6, 1866; J. N. Saénz to Negrete, Valladama, February 7, 1866, Antonio Ochoa to Juárez, Guadalupe y Calvo, June 2, 1866, in *ibid.* For an account and defense of Negrete's activities on behalf of González Ortega see Doroteo Negrete, *La verdad ante la figura militar de don Miguel Negrete* (Puebla, 1936), pp. 187-188.

30. An extremely lengthy and complete defense of González Ortega's claim to the presidency and the men who supported him appears in a letter from Prieto to his friends, San Antonio, September 9, 1866, in González Ortega Typescripts, V. See also Prieto to Mateos, San Antonio, June 4, 1866, in *Diario imperio,* July 28, 1866; Prieto to Negrete, San Antonio, May 6 and 11, 1866, in *Mex. Leg. Corresp.,* VIII, 518-519.

31. Unaddressed letter from Prieto, San Antonio, May 6, 1866, in *Diario imperio,* August 7, 1866. An unidentified letter written from Monterrey to Chihuahua August 26, 1866, reported that Prieto had written for permission to return to the Juárez fold and had been directed to apply directly to Juarez for this permission. *Mex. Leg. Corresp.,* VIII, 523.

32. Romero to Minister of Foreign Relations, Washington, December 22, 1866, in *Mex. Leg. Corresp.,* VIII, 799-780, and various other letters in *Corresp. conducta* written during 1866.

33. McKee to Iglesias, New York, August 28, 1866, in *Periodico Oficial,* November 3, 1866. This letter also contains a copy of the agreement with González Ortega dated July 24, 1866. Iglesias to McKee, Chihuahua, October 29, 1866, in *ibid.* contains a refusal of McKee's request.

34. Galindo y Galindo, *Gran década,* III, 526. See also Bancroft, *Mexico,* VI, 229, and Beals, *Diaz,* p. 151.

35. Bulnes, *El verdadero Juárez,* pp. 695-696; Zamacois, *Historia de*

Méjico, XVIII, 631; Vigil, *Reforma,* pp. 797-798; Sierra, *Juárez,* p. 453. In a conversation between the French minister in the United States and the Secretary of State the former asserted that all the French wanted was a stable government in Mexico under González Ortega or anyone else, but that González Ortega seemed logical and "we have in regard to him no bias or prejudice." *Diario oficial,* November 24, 1867. See also letters from Romero, December 7, 1866, and February 9, 1867, in *Mex. Leg. Corresp.,* VIII, 707 and IX, 116-117.

36. Cited in Roeder, *Juárez,* II, 648. Corti, *Maximilian,* II, 742-743, says that González Ortega was an impossible choice for the French by the fall of 1866.
37. Cited in González Ortega, *Golpe,* p. 360.
38. González Ortega to Sheridan, October 29, 1866, in *Corresp. conducta,* pp. 179-180.
39. Drew to Paulson, Brazos, November 3, 1866, in González Ortega, *Golpe,* p. 361.
40. González Ortega to Paulson, Brazos, November 5, 1866, in *ibid.*
41. J. González Ortega, Fernando María Ortega, E. Huerta, Juan Togno, Joaquín González Ortega, Carlos L. Ortega and Francisco Guiliaza to Colonel Charles H. Morse, Brazos, November 25 and December 3, 1866, in *ibid.,* pp. 364-367.
42. *Ibid.,* p. 355.
43. This action was anticipated by Sheridan in New Orleans, but no move was made to prevent it. Sheridan to Grant, November 27 and 30, 1866; Stanton to Sheridan, November 30, 1866, in U. S. Department of State *Papers,* 39 Cong., 2 Sess. (1866-1867), III, 422-423. Sedgwick apparently had been taken in by the foreign merchants in Matamoros who wished to secure funds due them from Canales before the town was taken by the Juarista forces. These merchants had been supporting Canales and reimbursing themselves by passing goods out of the city free or nearly free of duty. Sheridan to Rawlins, December 11, 1866, in U. S. *House Executive Documents,* 39 Cong., 2 Sess. (1866-1867), No. 17, 177-178; Sheridan to Grant, December 10, 1866, in *ibid.,* No. 76, 545.
44. Seward to Romero, December 17, 1866, in U. S. Department of State *Papers,* 40 Cong., 2 Sess. (1867-1868), No. 1, II, 500; Zamacois, *Historia de Méjico,* XVIII, 714; González Ortega, *Golpe,* pp. 357-359.
45. Sheridan to Grant, December 11, 1866, in U. S. *House Executive Documents,* 39 Cong., 2 Sess. (1866-1867), No. 76, 546. See also P. H. Sheridan, *Personal Memoirs* (New York, 1888, 2 vols.), II,

223-224.
46. *Mex. Leg. Corresp.,* IX, 82-90. The place in which this manifesto was written is not given. The American consul in Mexico City reported that this protest "caused some impression, and, skillfully used, may lead to an understanding between this general and the present ministry, which, in the event of Maximilian's abdication, would readily unite with González Ortega, from whom they expect to gain immunity from the past and security for the future." Marcus Otterbuty to Seward, January 17, 1867, in U. S. Department of State *Papers,* 40 Cong., 2 Sess., (1867-1868), No. 1, II, 345-347. At the same time support for Juárez was announced from various points in Mexico. See for example, the pronouncement by more than 70 officers of Huasichinango of January 4, 1867, in *La Soberania de Tamaulipas,* January 16, 1867.
47. M. Auza to Minister of *Gobernación,* Zacatecas, January 8, 1867, in *Colección de leyes,* pp. 124-125. Lerdo to Auza, January 10, 1867, in *ibid.,* p. 152, commends the governor's action and offers further justification for the arrest order. See also Juárez, *Archivos privados,* p. 200.
48. Roeder, *Juárez,* II, 655-673; Bancroft, *Mexico,* VI, 264-320. It is interesting that Maximilian, in disclaiming the right of a military court to try him, compared his situation with that of González Ortega. Maximilian to Escobedo, Querétaro, May 29, 1867, in Arias, *Reseña historia,*pp. 358-359. Maximilian pointed out that both had been imprisoned, but that González Ortega was evidently being held for trial by a proper tribunal. Furthermore Maximilian stated that his government, in contrast with González Ortega's, had been recognized by some foreign powers and had occupied Mexican territory, so that he even more than González Ortega deserved trial by some authority other than the military.
49. Bancroft,*Mexico,* VI, 333-348; Roeder, *Juárez,* II, 677.
50. D y L, *Legislacion,* X, 44-49; Roeder, *Juárez,* II, 682.
51. Scholes, *Juárez,* pp. 118-122; Bancroft, *Mexico,* VI, 354-355. The proposed reforms included the veto power for the president, the creation of an upper house in Congress, qualification for federal employees to stand for election to Congress, and suffrage for the clergy.
52. *El Globo de México,* December 19, 1867. Juárez received 7,422 electoral votes to 2,709 for Díaz. The fact that González Ortega ran third with 57 votes indicates that there was still some support for him, but at the same time it indicates how weak this support really was.

53. D y L, *Legislación,* X, 217, 219.
54. In protest against González Ortega's prolonged imprisonment, a few of his faithful friends in his old home, Tlaltenango, elected him to Congress, but the election was ignored. Carlos R. Ibarra to González Ortega, Tlaltenango, October 10, 1867, in González Ortega Typescripts, V. See also Daniel Cosío Villegas, *Historia moderna de México* (México, 1955, 8 vols.), I, 200.

IX
Freedom and Retirement

At the beginning of March, 1867, González Ortega was moved from Saltillo to Monterrey, where he remained during the rest of his period of imprisonment. Only persons above suspicion were allowed to visit him, and his correspondence was closely watched.[1] By the summer of 1867 he evidently gave up any hope of winning his dispute with Juárez, but he still looked upon himself as a martyr to the cause of legality. The letters which he wrote to his son in Philadelphia displayed a considerable amount of bitterness toward Juárez and disappointment in the Mexican people for not rallying to his support.[2]

Although González Ortega expressed the belief that he would be freed as soon as the empire was completely defeated, he was informed in August that the government still anticipated trying him for his crimes, but that action was being postponed until after the elections. At the same time the administration reasserted its right to hold him and try him in view of the special powers given to the president during the war.[3] He answered this communication by pointing to his previous protests, which he maintained disproved the administration's allegations that he was guilty of crimes against the state and that it had any legal right to act against him. He added that Juárez was wrong in assuming that acceptance of his own acts made them right. To support this argument he quoted from Alexis de Tocqueville's *Democracy in America* the statement that it was incorrect to assume that the fact of obedience gave to those obeyed the right of command.[4]

Gómez forwarded González Ortega's letter to Juárez with the recommendation that it be published along with a strong reply.[5] Soon afterward, in spite of the close watch kept on González Ortega, this letter appeared in various newspapers throughout Mexico. Gómez informed the administration of this fact and again urged that the government issue a strong reply. Juárez evidently planned to act on this advice, but there is no evidence that he did so.[6]

The whole question of González Ortega's imprisonment and claim to the presidency now began to receive considerable attention in the national press, particularly in newspapers that were hostile to Juárez. Following the announcement of Juárez' election the opposition press, led by *El Globo de Mexico,* announced that the time had come to expose the entire González Ortega affair. It explained that the subject had not been brought up before because of the dangers involved while the nation was at war. For the same reason action had been delayed until after national elections had been held.[7]

On December 8, 1867, González Ortega addressed a communication to the national congress and to various newspapers in the capital accusing Juárez of violating the constitution and calling for some action on his own arbitrary imprisonment. Evidently his guards prevented this letter from reaching all of those to whom it was addressed,[8] but enough copies of the protest reached congress to bring about approval of an order for a judicial investigation of the case.[9] The fact that no action was taken would seem to substantiate the charge of arbitrary imprisonment so often raised by the González Ortega partisans.

These evasions by the government gave the opposition press additional opportunities to embarass the administration. On December 24, 1867, *El Globo de México* published a lengthy article by Prieto, dated at San Antonio, September 17, 1866, which set forth the usual arguments in defense of González Ortega.[10] Beginning with the December 26 issue this same newspaper published the two protests González Ortega had issued at Eagle Pass and San Antonio in December 1866.[11] On January 19, 1868, another defense of González Ortega appeared in *El Globo de México* in the form of a letter to the editors from his various friends in Zacatecas. It reviewed his actions and quoted the constitution to show that he should have been president. The letter concluded with a condemnation of Juárez and a request that he be freed so that he could return to Zacatecas.[12]

During February and March, 1868, the discussion of González Ortega's imprisonment continued in the anti-Juárez newspapers. It was pointed out that under the constitution those judges elected in 1862 served until May, 1868; and that according to the special privileges given to these judges under the constitution, only congress had the right to accuse one of them of a crime.[13] Various rumors concerning González Ortega circulated; that he would be freed by the government, that he had accepted terms from the administration in exchange for complete and unconditional freedom, and that he would be returned to the presidency of the court.[14] In general, however, the opposition press complained most about the lack of any definite action by the government. It was not the imprisonment of González Ortega that bothered them but the arbitrary manner in which it was carried out.

In March González Ortega again circulated the request for an investigation by congress which he had first issued in December 1867. In an accompanying letter to the editors of *El Globo de México,* he explained that he was not certain his first request had been received since he was held virtually incommunicado.[15] The newspaper published his complete letter along with most of the documents which were included. These consisted of a complete resume of his actions since 1864, with a detailed account of his arrest in the United States. Also included was information concerning what he had published from time to time and where these publications could be located.[16]

This new petition was discussed in a secret session of congress and passed to the committee on petitions for consideration. The point was raised that since González Ortega claimed that the acting government of Mexico, including the congress was illegal, it was inconsistent for him to direct a petition to that body asking for an investigation of his case.[17] Matías Romero, now a member of the cabinet, replied to the petition by publishing a few documents relative to the Matamoros affair and González Ortega's imprisonment in the United States.[18] This was a direct result of charges that the petition brought against Romero. He alleged that Romero had not opposed American intervention in the internal affairs of Mexico, but had actually sought that intervention. The papers Romero supplied were routine documents that failed to answer González Ortega's charges.

On May 6, in a letter to the editors of the official publication of Nuevo León, González Ortega explained his reasons for addressing a legislative body which he considered to be illegal. He stated that since the coup d'etat at Paso del Norte he did not recognize Juárez' authority or any of his acts. He could not, therefore, recognize Juárez' right to call an election for the national congress, but at the same time he could and did recognize the members of this congress as representatives of the people, especially since they were meeting in accordance with the constitution and not as a revolutionary body. He explained that he felt obligated to direct himself to the representatives of the people.[19]

González Ortega's letter added that the only purpose for the debate was to arrive at the truth by legal means. He stated that a revolution against Juárez would be bad for the country, since it would show that force was Mexico's only tribunal. He asserted that he himself had no intention of causing trouble. His only reason for petitioning congress was to have his rights recognized so that he could resign his office. This, he said, was his duty, for the people of Mexico had elected him to an office and he could not give it up except in accordance with the law. He concluded with the promise that he had not authorized and would not authorize any disturbance in his name and, even more, he would not consider leading such an uprising.

The reference to disturbances in González Ortega's name was undoubtedly included to remove him from any connection with recent pronouncements by various discontented Liberals who had used his cause as an excuse to rebel. The most outstanding of these were probably Miguel Negrete and Aureliano Rivera, who had placed themselves in armed opposition to Juárez shortly after González Ortega sent his petition to congress. Negrete was still anxious to restore himself to favor in Mexico, and he saw no chance of doing so with Juárez in office. Rivera evidently operated on the principle that a true liberal must revolt against authority, and the authority in this case was Juárez.[20] The actions between these insurgents and the government troops never assumed the proportions of battles, and Rivera and Negrete were forced to flee from Mexico within a few months. Other less important rebels met a similar fate, but not before they had caused the administration some discomfort.[21]

These armed actions in González Ortega's name, according to *El Globo de México,* prevented any public demonstration when Lerdo announced to the permanent deputation of congress that he was replacing González Ortega as president of the supreme court. The paper explained that many persons refrained from protesting more vigorously the unlawful act against González Ortega in order to avoid lending moral aid to the movements by Negrete and others.[22] The question of González Ortega's imprisonment continued to receive attention in the press, however. It was rumored, and probably with some basis in fact, that he had been removed from the house in which he had been held prisoner to the public jail in Monterrey, and that many privileges which he had enjoyed were taken away as a result of the various communications which he had managed to send out to congress and to the press.[23] The primary issue was still not the fact that he was in prison but that he had been imprisoned arbitrarily, without trial.[24]

Probably as a result of the increasing embarassment that González Ortega caused the administration, and because he was no longer dangerous, the government ordered his release on July 18, 1868. In ordering his freedom, however, the government left an opening for future action against him. The official order from Mejía to the governor of Nuevo León explained that congress had the right to try him for desertion of his post as chief justice of the supreme court, and that he could be tried by a civil judge for desertion of his army post.[25] Since congress had delayed action on the first crime, the government had taken no action on the common crime of desertion. Should congress decide to try him, however, the government would follow with a trial for the second crime. It was also explained that he had been kept in prison without a trial because of the danger to the government which his freedom would have implied. Now that the danger had passed, he was to be freed.

Freeing González Ortega did not end discussion of the issue. Editorials continued to attack Juárez for arbitrary actions and to express fear that other unconstitutional moves might be made. They expressed approval of the extension of Juárez' term of office in 1865, but pointed out he had bypassed the constitution more than had really been necessary. These editorials were not pro-González Ortega, nor were they intended to be. They simply emphasized the separation of executive and judicial powers so that Juárez would not be tempted to continue acting outside the constitution.[26]

González Ortega and Patoni were actually freed on August 2, 1868, and Patoni left for Durango. González Ortega remained at Monterrey for a few days before moving to Saltillo.[27] Shortly after his arrival in Durango, Patoni was killed under circumstances which cast suspicion on the Juárez government, although subsequent investigations revealed nothing which could be construed as governmental approval of the assassination.[28] The officer in charge of the troops responsible for Patoni's death was summoned to Mexico City to stand trial. The attitude of some people toward the assassination can be judged from the actions of González Ortega's partisans in Zacatecas when the accused officer passed through that town en route to the capital. Fights broke out between the local citizens and the federal troops, with cries of death to Juárez and death to González Ortega being exchanged.[29] While the citizens of Zacatecas were undoubtedly more inclined to support González Ortega than were most Mexicans, the suspicion of the government was certainly not localized.

On August 19, 1868, at Saltillo, González Ortega issued a manifesto to the Mexican nation which dealt a death blow to any revolutionary movement in his name. He stated that he had been thinking over the events of the past years and the present status of the government. In view of the general acceptance of Juárez and the normal operation of his government, he continued, there was little left for him to do but accept also. He explained that his supporters had gradually disappeared, leaving him alone, and that most of the outstanding liberals had joined the Juárez administration either actively or tacitly. As the only alternative to rebellion, he offered his resignation as constitutional president of the supreme court and interim president of the republic. He concluded with the assertion that he had been dominated by the highest motives during his public career.[30]

Following the appearance of this manifesto, González Ortega wrote to Juárez expressing his hope that the people of Mexico would accept it and offering his services to the government should they ever be needed. He also suggested that he might find it expedient to leave Mexico and make his home in some foreign country.[31] Juárez thanked him and assured him that there was no need to leave Mexico. He also informed González Ortega that should his services ever be required, he would certainly call on him and it "would not be, as you know very well, in a manner offensive to your personal security."[32] Before receiving this answer González Ortega again wrote to the president suggesting that it might be best if he left Mexico for a while, but that he lacked the necessary funds to make such a trip.[33] Juárez assured him that his request was modest, but that he did not wish to set a precedent and, as he had already stated, there was no reason for him to leave the country.[34]

A part of the Mexican press could not believe that González Ortega had given up the fight, especially when some citizens of Zacatecas proposed him as a candidate for governor of that state in October, 1868. His major opponent was Trinidad García de la Cadena, a popular leader and probably the real strong man of the state.[35] Rumors appeared to the effect that González Ortega was returning to Zacatecas to take an active part in the campaign, and the question of his eligibility was raised. It was pointed out that four years had not elapsed since he held the office of governor, and under the state constitution he was therefore ineligible to run.[36] González Ortega made no effort to secure his election, but neither did he express himself publicly as being opposed to the nomination.[37] When the election was held, however, García de la Cadena won 207 electoral votes to 132 for González Ortega.[38]

On December 2, González Ortega addressed a manifesto to his friends in Zacatecas explaining his actions in the election just held. He stated that he had intended to remain entirely out of public affairs after his declaration of the previous September, but he felt that he owed some explanation to those who had supported him for governor. He believed that he would be a hindrance to the Liberal party in Zacatecas because of the enemies he had acquired, and he denied emphatically the charge that he had ever sought public office simply out of a desire for power. He concluded with a plea for unanimous support of García de la Cadena and a request that he be left in peace from that time on.[39]

The request to be left out of politics went unheeded in Zacatecas, however, for a faction was organized to oppose Juárez and his candidates for state offices. At the state convention in June, 1869, González Ortega was nominated as the "people's candidate" for deputy to the state legislature, and when the elections were over he had won absolute majorities in the districts of both Zacatecas and Tlaltenango.[40] At the same time he was elected as a state representative to the national congress.[41] Although he made no move to accept these offices, it was seriously expected at the time that he would come out of retirement.[42]

A general epidemic of minor revolts against Juárez culminated in January, 1870, with an organized movement headed by

132

Governor García de la Cadena of Zacatecas, and once again González Ortega was involved involuntarily in national affairs.[43] This revolt, which developed in the states of San Luis Potosi, Zacatecas, Jalisco, and Querétaro, adopted as its political goal the overthrow of Juárez and the recognition of González Ortega as president because of the illegality of the November 8 decrees by Juárez.[44]

Once again González Ortega felt compelled to break his self-imposed silence, and on January 22, 1870, one month before the revolutionary movement was crushed, he addressed another manifesto to the citizens of Zacatecas. In this document he expressed surprise that anyone would use his claim for the presidency as an excuse for revolting against the government, since he had already resigned all powers which he had held. Even when he held the presidency of the court, he added, he had never advocated the use of force, but had maintained his argument on the basis of constitutional principles. He concluded with the assertion that he had never been consulted concerning the revolt and that the insurgents had no reason to involve him.[45] The appearance of this manifesto was applauded throughout the country since many persons believed that he had been waiting for an opportunity to lead a revolutionary movement. This was the last time that González Ortega was ever suspected of designs on the presidency either legally or otherwise.

One further public utterance by González Ortega appeared in 1871 when elections were being held to determine the president of Mexico for the next four years. The leading candidates were Juárez, Lerdo, and Díaz. The charges hurled against Juárez were numerous, and Díaz had gained the support of leading Liberals who had formerly supported Juárez.[46] González Ortega, who took no part in the election, was called upon by the press and by personal friends to voice some preference of candidates, and on May 6, 1871, he issued a rather backhanded endorsement of Juárez, stating that in view of the existing circumstances he was inclined to favor Juárez, "not to reward his antecedents, but in order to avoid new conflicts for Mexico." He admitted that Lerdo was intelligent, but he felt that Lerdo's talents were nullified by his behavior. Díaz, he said, in probably one of the greatest understatements of his career, had given good service but did not have the necessary stature. He again voiced his partiality for Juárez because Juárez had demonstrated his ability to hold the country together for the past fourteen years under difficult circumstances.

Although this statement may well have been interpreted as an insult to Juárez in its implication that if Juárez were defeated, an armed revolt might follow, the Juarista faction accepted it as a sign of support and publicized it as such. As events turned out, a revolt occurred despite the fact that Juárez had won.[47] On October 12 the congress declared that Juárez had been elected, and on November 7 Díaz began an unsuccessful revolt.[48]

González Ortega continued living in retirement at Saltillo, and although he lived through the death of Juárez in July, 1872, the administration of Lerdo, and the subsequent rise of Díaz, he not only refused to discuss politics in public but apparently even ceased to keep up with current events in Mexico. For more than a decade he stayed at Saltillo, dominated by what one writer has called misanthropy.[49] He cut off relations with all those who were not members of his immediate family and devoted himself exclusively to study and writing. What income he had, and it must have been quite modest, was derived from various interests which he still held in Zacatecas. His sister managed these interests until his son returned from the United States some time after González Ortega's release from prison.[50]

Evidently González Ortega had acquired one of the finest libraries in Mexico, and he frequently wrote his son for books for this library.[51] As a result of his studies and meditations he produced a number of essays on general history, philosophy, and principally on the speculative principles of religion.[52] An indication of his concern with religious matters is seen in a partial list of books which his son sent to Saltillo. Among these were Mazo's

History of Religion, Cobbett's *History of the Protestant Reform,* Veuillot's *Library of Religion,* Marquez' *Summary of Ecclesiastical History,* Horace in Latin, Virgil in Latin, *Sacred Books of the Orient,* Malebranch's *Inquiries Concerning the Truth,* Boubier's *Theological Institutions,* and Saint Thomas' *Summa Theologica.* Other books were on geography, history, astronomy, anatomy, legislation, philosophy, and chemistry. It is significant that none of the books he requested or any of his writings were concerned with contemporary Mexican history.[53]

González Ortega also wrote a series of letters to his son on religious subjects. The following paragraph taken from one of these will show the type of problem with which he was dealing:

> You will remain more convinced of this last truth, if you agree to the former; that according to the conscience of Christ, he was of the same nature as [illegible word], as Simon the magician, as the young man of Tyre, and as all men in general. And I say according to the conscience of Christ, because Christ was not an imposter, but a great Prophet, and we ought to hold his statement as the expression of his true conscience, and Christ neither believed nor said that he was God; on the contrary, he said that he was the Son of Man, and he spoke of God as of another person distinct from him, and of a nature also distinct. And if sometimes he said he was the Son of God, it was in the same manner in which we all say it, because we find ourselves in the same condition as Christ, as creatures formed by the hands of the Supreme Creator. Among the many texts from the sacred books which could be used to prove this, I select only one in order not to make this letter too long: "Then a young man approached him and said unto him: Good Master, what must I do in order to gain eternal life? Jesus replied to him: Why do you call me good? Only God is good. If you wish to gain eternal life, obey the commandments." St. Matthew, Chap. XIX, 16 and 17; St.

Mark, Chap. X, 17 and 18; St. Luke, Chap. XVIII, 18 and 19.[54]

Throughout the years of his retirement González Ortega was almost forgotten by the Mexican people and the government. In January, 1881, however, President Manuel González heeded the request of Secretary of War Geronimo Treviño, and restored González Ortega to his former rank as a general of the Mexican army.[55] This, the president stated in a letter to González Ortega, satisfied "a debt of gratitude to the military leader of the Reform and to the heroic defender of his country's soil against the foreign invader."[56]

A little over a month after this recognition González Ortega became ill, and on February 28, 1881, he died at his home in Saltillo. His body was embalmed and in March was conducted to Zacatecas with military honors. After a ceremony honoring him in his native state, his body was removed at the direction of President González to the rotunda of the Panteón de Dolores in Mexico City, where it was buried alongside the graves of other illustrious men in Mexican history.[57] Thus ended the career of "the spoiled son of Zacatecas, the sustainer of its liberties, the champion of the Reform, the savior of the Independence of the Fatherland," General of Division Jesús González Ortega.[58]

NOTES

1. González Ortega to Laurito, Monterry, June 18, 1867, in González Ortega, *Golpe,* pp. 376-378.
2. *Ibid.* See also various poems which González Ortega wrote while at Monterrey and sent to his son, in González Ortega Typescripts, V. In one of these González Ortega compared himself to Aristides of ancient Athens, who was likewise rejected by his contemporaries only to achieve his true place in history as a great man. Álvarez, *Estudios,* pp. 186-187, compares him to Nebuchadnezzar, who enjoyed great popularity until the soberness of man and the hand of God reduced him to public scorn.

3. Mejía to Manuel Z. Gómez, Mexico, August 16, 1867, in González Ortega, *Golpe,* pp. 378-379. Gómez was the military commander of the state of Nuevo Leon and the official directly responsible for holding González Ortega in prison.
4. *Ibid.,* pp. 369-372, 380-383.
5. Gómez to Juárez, Monterrey, September 24, 1867, in Archivo Juárez Manuscripts.
6. Gómez to Juárez, November 26, 1867, in *ibid.* A note in Juárez' handwriting at the top of this letter indicates his approval of Gómez' suggestion.
7. *El Globo de México,* December 2, 1867; Zamacois, *Historia de Méjico,* XX, 126.
8. *El Globo,* April 16, 1868; González Ortega, *Golpe,* p. 383. It is quite possible that the documents sent out by González Ortega did reach the newspapers, but were not published at the time. *Diario Oficial,* April 23, 1868.
9. Gibaja y Patrón, *Comentario,* V, 338; Roeder, *Juárez,* II, 687.
10. On the following day Prieto wrote to González Ortega telling him that he was working to save his honor. González Ortega Manuscripts.
11. *El Globo,* December 26, 1867, to January 7, 1868.
12. Some friends of General González Ortega to editors of *El Globo,* Zacatecas, January 5, 1868.
13. *El Globo,* February 12 and 13, 1868. Lerdo gave the administration's answer to the various newspaper charges. *El Siglo XIX,* February 27, 1868.
14. *El Ferrocarril,* no date, cited in *El Globo,* February 14, 1868; *The Two Republics,* no date, cited in *ibid.,* April 9, 1868; *Democrata,* no date, cited in *ibid,* March 27, 1868.
15. April 16, 1868.
16. April 16 to 19, 1868.
17. *Diario Oficial,* April 18, 1868, and *Le Trait d'Union,* no date, cited in *El Globo,* April 23, 1868.
18. *El Globo,* April 20, 1868.
19. González Ortega to editors of *Periódico Oficial de Nuevo León,* Monterrey, May 6, 1868, in *ibid.,* May 24, 1868.
20. Zamacois, *Historia de Méjico,* XIX, 418, 424-439; *Diario Oficial,* April 23, 1868.
21. Zamacois, *Historia de Méjico,* XX, 22; Bancroft, *Mexico,* VI, 365-366.
22. June 6 and 9, 1868. The danger of armed uprising in the name of González Ortega was at least one reason for the passage by congress

in April, 1868, of a law giving the president extraordinary powers to punish conspirators against the government. Zamacona and other anti-Juárez leaders opposed it unsuccessfully. Certainly it was to the advantage of the opponents of Juárez to exploit the González Ortega affair in an attempt to embarass the administration, but it was undesirable to have the danger from González Ortega seem so great that Juárez might be justified in more dictatorial action. Cosío Villegas, *Historia moderna,* I, 241-243.

23. *El Monitor Republicano,* no date, cited in *El Globo,* July 9, 1868.
24. *Grano de Arena,* no date, cited in *ibid.,* July 1, 1868.
25. Secretary of State to governor of Nuevo León, Mexico, July 18, 1868, in *Diario Oficial,* July 21, 1868. Patoni had been offered his freedom in September if he would agree to come to Mexico City and await trial. Patoni had refused to accept anything other than unconditional freedom. Mejía to governor of Nuevo León, Mexico, September 6, 1867; Patoni to Gómez, Monterrey, September 23, 1867, in *ibid.* See also *El Globo,* July 28, 1868.
26. *El Globo* July 26 and 30, August 5, 1868.
27. *Ibid.,* August 16 and 18, 1868. González Ortega was seriously considering leaving Mexico to insure peace and his own personal safety. González Ortega to Cosío, Saltillo, August 6, 1868, in *Defensor de la Reforma,* September 15, 1868.
28. The exact circumstances surrounding Patoni's death are somewhat uncertain, but it would appear that a small group of the state militia of Durango took him from his home to the outskirts of town and shot him. This is the story reported in various letters from Durango in *El Globo,* August 26, 1868. One theory concerning Patoni's death which may very well have been true was that he was killed by friends of the former Miguel Cruz-Aedo, a local hero who was believed to have been killed during the War of the Reform at the orders of Patoni and González Ortega. *La Paz,* no date, in *ibid.,* September 12, 1868. See above, Chapter II.
29. Zamacois, *Historia de Méjico,* XX, 226; González Ortega, *Golpe,* p. 385.
30. González Ortega to the Mexican Nation, Saltillo, August 19, 1868, in González Ortega Typescripts, V. Negrete attempted to persuade González Ortega not to give up but learned that he was seriously ill. Negrete, *La Verdad,* p. 214. Apparently González Ortega suffered from rheumatism during the years following his imprisonment. *El Pajaro Verde,* no date, in *ibid.,* p. 195.
31. Saltillo, August 31, 1868, in Archivo Juárez Manuscripts.
32. September 14, 1868, in *ibid.*

33. September 9, 1868, in *ibid.*
34. September 22, 1868, in *ibid.* It has been suggested that González Ortega issued his manifesto and decided to leave Mexico because he feared for his own life after the assassination of Patoni. There does not appear to be any foundation in this suggestion, however. See González Ortega, *Golpe,* p. 385, and Rivera, *Anales,* p. 291. See also *La Iberia,* no date, cited in *El Monitor Republicano,* October 8, 1868.
35. *La Linterna Mágica,* no date, cited in *El Globo,* October 19, 1868; González Ortega, *Golpe,* p. 391. Zamacona called González Ortega's manifesto an "important triumph of government and legal order," and gave up any fight in the name of González Ortega. Cosío Villegas, *Historia Moderna,* I, 371.
36. *El Globo,* October 19 and 29, 1868.
37. González Ortega, *Golpe,* 391, states that he wrote privately to some friends declining the governorship.
38. *El Monitor Republicano,* November 7, 1868.
39. González Ortega to friends in the state of Zacatecas, Saltillo, December 2, 1868, in González Ortega Typescripts, V, and *El Monitor Republicano,* December 19, 1868.
40. Electoral College of Tlaltenango to González Ortega, July 11, 1869. in González Ortega Manuscripts; *El Globo,* June 1, 9, July 20, September 15 and 17, 1869.
41. *El Globo,* August 2 and 31, 1869.
42. *Regeneración Social,* no date, cited in *ibid.,* August 5, 1869.
43. Zamacois, *Historia de Méjico,* XXI, 124-129; Bancroft, *Mexico,* VI, 372-374.
44. This revolution has been attributed to Juárez' attempts to retain power and to the unparalled cruelties of government officers in that year; but evidently there was a certain amount of personal ambition involved. Bancroft, *Mexico,* VI, 373-374. This revolt was based upon the Plan of San Luis issued on December 30, 1869, by García de la Cadena and Ireneo Paz. Under this plan (1) the army was to be reduced in size, (2) federal powers were to be reestablished at a central location, (3) the decrees of November 8, 1865, were declared void, (4) González Ortega was to be the legal president, and (5) if he refused, some other justice would assume the presidency. Cosío Villegas, *Historia moderna,* I, 553-555.
45. González Ortega to his fellow citizens, Saltillo, January 22, 1870, in Zamacois, *Historia de Méjico,* XXI, 257-260.
46. Walter V. Scholes, "El Mensajero and the Election of 1871 in Mexico," *The Americas* (July, 1848), 61. This article presents many

of the charges which were brought against Juárez by a pro-Díaz newspaper.

47. González Ortega, *Golpe,* pp. 393-394.
48. Scholes, "El Mensajero," p. 67.
49. Rivera, *Anales,,* p. 291.
50. González Ortega, *Golpe,* p. 389.
51. Bancroft Manuscripts, Notes on Mexico in 1883, University of California; González Ortega, *Golpe,* p. 389. This library along with that of Gómez Farías today makes up a large part of the public library of Zacatecas.
52. These writings were never published and the present writer has been unable to obtain the originals or copies of them.
53. González Ortega, *Golpe,* p. 389.
54. Cited in *ibid.,* pp. 389-390.
55. Trevino to González Ortega, Mexico, January 6, 1881, in *ibid.,* p. 399.
56. González to González Ortega, Mexico, January 13, 1881, in *ibid.* See also Bulnes, *Juárez y las revoluciones,* p. 615.
57. González Ortega, *Golpe,* p. 399; Miguel Angel Peral, *Diccionario biográfico mexicano* (México, no date), p. 350.
58. *Discurso pronunciado en la Alameda de Zacatecas el 14 de marzo de 1881, por el Lic. Trinidad García de la Cadena, en los honores funebres tributados al Benemerito General de División C. Jesús González Ortega* (Zacatecas, 1881), cited in González Ortega, *Golpe,* p. 400.

X
Epilogue

Each generation in a nation's history produces a few men whose names are inseparable from that history. Some of these men attain their places in history because of their accomplishments; others, because of their failures. González Ortega must be counted among those who are remembered because of their achievements and in spite of their failures. His importance to Mexico cannot be ignored when it is remembered that his lifetime encompassed one of the most significant periods in that nation's history. For more than a decade he was intimately associated with the national politics of Mexico, and even when his active political life was over, his name remained a symbol with which to conjure up revolution.

Although the final judgment on his life is yet to be made, some things are apparent with regard to his role in Mexican national politics. His early association with the Liberal cause in Zacatecas was one of his first steps on the road to national prominence, although his moderate position in the election of 1857 belies to some extent the radical stamp which is usually applied to him.

At the beginning of the War of the Reform González Ortega demonstrated that he was a man who could act in support of the Liberal principles which he had been advancing in his writings and speeches. Seizing control of the state government, he organized men and resources for the battle against the Conservative forces, and in the process established himself as a leading target of the clerical groups in Mexico. He also anticipated the action of the national government and decreed many of the Laws of the Reform before their enactment for all of Mexico.

The lack of complete information on González Ortega's early life makes it impossible to determine what factors contributed to the formation of his political convictions, although it is safe to assume that the friends he made as a journalist and aspiring young politician influenced him to some extent. His relatively sudden rise to prominence can be explained only on the basis of personal attraction and the unsettled conditions of Mexico at the time.

Taking the field as a military leader in 1859, González Ortega soon established himself as one of the most important men in the Liberal camp. After significant victories at Peñuelas and Silao, he led the victorious Mexican army on the plains of Calpulalpam in the final major battle of the war. In December, 1860, he entered Mexico City at the head of 25,000 men as the hero of the hour and, although few similar acts had ever been performed in Mexican history, turned the reins of government over to the legitimate president.

In the reconstruction period following the war González Ortega was rewarded for his services by election to the presidency of the supreme court. During this same period his personal conflict with Juárez became apparent, but even though other opponents of Juárez attempted to make the conflict more serious, he did not support them. He continued to serve his country in the military sphere, although his effectiveness during this period was hampered by the quarrel with Juárez.

During the period of the intervention González Ortega earned a reputation as a military leader which reached the capitals of Europe. The siege of Puebla, in spite of the conflicting reports about it, remains one of the most outstanding examples of military valor in modern history. His actions in 1864 indicate that he, like other Liberals at that time, was beginning to despair of the chances for victory. His attempt to force Juárez' resignation with the flimsy excuse that the French would not treat with him, and his letter relative to the end of Juárez' term of office in 1864 are both difficult to understand. Possibly he actually believed that if he were president some agreement could be reached with the French, but at the same time these actions were hardly proper in view of the critical situation of the government.

González Ortega's explanation for his departure to the United States and his prolonged stay in that country seem plausible enough on the surface, but it is to be suspected that once he reached the United States he was influenced considerably by other Mexican residents in that country. In December, 1865, he became the legal president of Mexico, for on the basis of the constitution there can be no doubt that his claim was legitimate. At the same time it is equally clear that Juárez was justified in prolonging his own term of office, and the fact that the majority of the Mexican people supported him and even re-elected him makes it clear that González Ortega was either politically inept or deceived about the state of affairs in Mexico.

The intervention of the United States in this conflict and González Ortega's arbitrary imprisonment after his return to Mexico are clearly unjustifiable. It is to be doubted whether he could have caused Juárez as much trouble free as he did in prison, for his imprisonment was a strong weapon in the hands of the opposition. It must also be pointed out to his credit that he continually disassociated himself from any armed attempt to overthrow Juárez.

González Ortega's attitude following his release from prison may perhaps be understandable, but it is unfortunate that a man of his demonstrated ability and popular appeal saw fit to withdraw completely from the political arena.

A true evaluation of González Ortega's service to his country is complicated by the presence of Benito Juárez. Juárez appeared as a symbol of the Liberal ideas to most of his countrymen, and the passing years have only served to glorify the memory of the humble Indian from Oaxaca. González Ortega suffers by comparison, yet it must be remembered that Juarez was not the only figure in the War of the Reform and the defeat of the empire. González Ortega, in his own field of activity, deserves as much attention as Juárez.

Even though it is true that a comparison of González Ortega and Juárez does not offer a sound basis for evaluation, the comparison is inescapable in view of the fact that González Ortega's political life was cut short by the actions of Juárez. Therein lies the tragedy of González Ortega's life. Juárez cannot be criticized, and in fact may even deserve praise, for recognizing reality in 1865 and acting according to the dictates of existing conditions for the good of Mexico. At the same time González Ortega cannot be condemned for ignoring his own common sense and insisting on the observance of the very laws for which he had fought. Regardless of the fact that this conflict can never be completely resolved, his career suffered as a result of it and the luster of his services to Mexico were dimmed in the process.

The historian, Francisco G. Cosmes, probably came close to the truth when he stated that history would do González Ortega justice by considering him "as one of the most handsome and, up to a certain point, pure figures that appeared on the public scene between 1859 and 1863."[1]

NOTES

1. Zamacois, *Historia de Méjico,* XXI, 264.

Bibliography
Sources

I   Manuscripts and Typescripts

Archivo Juárez, Biblioteca Nacional, Mexico City.
Bancroft Papers, University of California (Berkeley).
Ignacio Comonfort Papers, University of Texas.
Santos Degollado Papers, Texas.
Manuel Doblado Typescripts, Texas.
Documentos relativos a la reforma, Texas.
Jesús González Ortega Papers, Texas.
Jesús González Ortega Typescripts, Texas.
Mariano Riva Palacio Papers, Texas.
Vicente Riva Palacio Papers, Texas.
Jesús Terán Typescripts, Texas.
Plácido Vega Papers, California.

II   Printed Documents and Correspondence

Archivo Mexicano. Colección de leyes, decretos, circulares y otros documentos. 6 vols., México, 1856-1862.
Bianchi, A. G. (ed.), *Correspondencia de Juárez y Montluc.* México, 1905.
British and Foreign State Papers, 1860-1862.
Carreño, Alberto María (ed.), *Archivo del General Porfirio Díaz.* 2 vols., México, 1947-1951.
Castañeda, Carols E. (ed.), *La guerra de reforma según el archivo del General D. Manuel Doblado, 1857-1860. Nuevos documentos inéditos o muy raros para la historia de México,* III. San Antonio, 1930.
Circulares y otras publicaciones por la legación mexicana en Washington durante la guerra de intervención, 1862-1867. 2 vols., México, 1868.
Colección de leyes, decretos y circulares expedidas por el supremo gobierno de la república, 1863-1867. 3 vols., México, 1867.
Correspondencia ofciial [sic] de la legación mexicana en Washing-

ton con el ministerio de relaciones exteriores de la república y el Departamento de Estado de Washington sobre la conducta de D. Jesús González Ortega, 1865-1866. México, 1869.

Documentos para la historia contemporanea de México. 2 vols., Mexico, 1867-1868.

Dublán, Manuel, and Lozano, José María (eds.), Legislación mexicana o colección completa de las disposiciones legislativas expedidas desde la independencia de la república. 34 vols., México, 1876-1904.

Garcia, Genaro (ed.), Don Santos Degollado, sus manifiestos, campañas, destitución militar, enjuiciamiento, rehabilitación, muerte, funerales, y honores póstumos. Documentos inéditos o muy raros para la historia de México, XI. México, 1907.

_____, El sitio de Puebla en 1863 según los archivos de D. Ignacio Comonfort y de D. Juan Antonio de la Fuente. Documentos inéditos o muy raros para la historia de México, XXIII. México, 1909.

González Ortega, Jesús, Parte general que da al supremo gobierno de la nación respecto de la defensa de la plaza de Zaragoza el C. General Jesús González Ortega. Mexico, 1871.

Gutiérrez, Blas José, and Alatorre, Flores (eds.), Leyes de reforma, colección de las disposiciones que se conocen con este nombre publicadas desde el año de 1855 al de 1870. 2 vols., México, 1868-1870.

Manning, William R. (ed.), Diplomatic Correspondence of the United States. 12 vols., Washington, 1932-1939.

Peña y Reyes, Antonio de la (ed.), La labor diplomática de D. Manuel María de Zamacona como Secretario de Relaciones Exteriores. Archivo Histórico Diplomático Mexicano, XXVIII. México, 1928.

Pérez Lugo, J., La cuestión religiosa en México, recopilación de leyes, disposiciones legales y documentos para el estudio de este problema político. México, 1926.

Puig Casauranc, J. M. (ed.), Archivos privados de D. Benito Juárez y D. Pedro Santacilia. Mexico, 1928.

Pola, Ángel (ed.), Discursos y manifiestos de Benito Juárez. México, 1905.

_____, Miscelanea de Benito Juárez. México, 1906.

_____, Obras completas de D. Melchor Ocampo. 3 vols., México,

1900-1901.

Roel, Santiago (ed.), *Correspondencia particular de D. Santiago Viduarri.* Vol. I, Juárez-Vidaurri. Monterrey, 1946.

Romero, Matías (ed.), *Correspondencia de la legación mexicana en Washington durante la intervención extranjera, 1860-1868.* 10 vols., México, 1870-1892.

Ruiz, Manuel, *Exposición que el C. Lic. Manuel Ruiz, ministro constitucional de la suprema corte de justicia de la nación, presenta al soberano congreso de la unión.* México, 1868.

United States *House Executive Documents.*
    No. 100, 37 Cong., 2 Sess. Washington, 1862.
    No. 120, 37 Cong., 2 Sess. Washington, 1862.
    No. 54, 37 Cong., 3 Sess. Washington, 1863.
    No. 73, 39 Cong., 1 Sess. Washington, 1866.
    No. 1, 39 Cong., 2 Sess. Washington, 1867.
    No. 17, 39 Cong., 2 Sess. Washington, 1867.
    No. 76, 39 Cong., 2 Sess. Washington, 1867.
    No. 30, 40 Cong., 1 Sess. Washington, 1867.
    No. 1, 40 Cong., 2 Sess. Washington, 1867.

United States *Papers Relating to Foreign Affairs.*
    39 Cong., 2 Sess., III. Washington, 1867.
    40 Cong., 2 Sess., II. Washington, 1868.

War of the Rebellion. Vols. XXXIV, XLI. Washington, 1891, 1893.

Zarco, Francisco (ed.), *Historia del congreso extraordinario constituyente de 1856 y 1857.* 2 vols., México, 1857.

III Newspapers and Periodicals (unless otherwise designated they are from Mexico City).

El Boletín de Noticias, 1860-1861.

El Defensor de la Reforma (Zacatecas), 1864.

El Diario de Avisos, 1856-1860.

El Diario Oficial (including *Periódico Oficial* of the Intervention Period).

El Diario del Imperio, 1865-1866.

El Estandarte Nacional, 1856-1857.

El Globo de México, 1867-1869.

El Heraldo, 1855-1862.

Jesús González Ortega

El Monitor Republicano, 1868-1872.
El Pájaro Verde, 1861.
El Siglo Diez y Nueve, 1858-1863.
La Soberanía de Tamaulipas (Tampico), 1866.
La Sombra de García (Zacatecas), April 17, 1857-May 30, 1857.

IV Secondary Materials

Álvarez, Ignacio, *Estudios sobre la historia general de México.* 6 vols., Zacatecas, 1875-1877.

Amador, Elías, *Bosquejo histórico de Zacatecas.* 2 vols., Zacatecas, 1943.

Arias, Juan de Dios, *Reseña histórica de la formación y operaciones del cuerpo de ejército del norte durante la intervención francesa, sitio de Querétaro y noticias oficiales sobre la captura de Maximiliano, su proceso integro y su muerte.* México, 1967.

Arrowood, Flora R., "United States-Mexican Foreign Relations from 1867-1872. Unpublished M.A. thesis, University of Texas, 1934.

Arrangoiz, Francisco de Paula de, *Méjico desde 1808 hasta 1867.* 4 vols., Madrid, 1871-1872.

Baez, Victoriano D., *Episódios históricos de la guerra de la intervención y el segundo imperio.* Oaxaca, 1907.

Bancroft, Hubert Howe, *History of Mexico.* 6 vols., San Francisco, 1881-1888.

Baz, Juan José, *Artículos diversos de La Bandera Roja de Morelia.* México, 1861.

Beals, Carleton, *Porfirio Díaz, Dictator of Mexico.* Philadelphia, 1932.

Blasio, José L., *Maximilian Emperor of México. Memoirs of His Private Secretary.* New Haven, 1934.

Bravo Ugarte, José, *Historia de México.* Vol III, México, 1944.

Buenrostro, Felipe, *Historia del primero y segundo congresos constitucionales de la República Mexicana.* 9 vols., México, 1874-1882.

Bulnes, Francisco, *El verdadero Juárez y la verdad sobre la intervención y el imperio.* México, 1904.

_____, *Juárez y las revoluciones de Ayutla y de la Reforma.* México, 1905.

Burke, Ulick Ralph, *A Life of Benito Juárez, Constitutional President of Mexico*. London, 1894.

Cadenhead, Ivie E., "González Ortega and the Presidency of Mexico." *HAHR* (August, 1952), 331-346.

Caldwell, Edward M., "The War of 'La Reforma' in Mexico, 1858-1861." Unpublished PhD. thesis, University of Texas, 1935.

Callahan, James M., *American Foreign Policy in Mexican Relations*. New York, 1932.

Callcott, Wilfrid H., *Church and State in Mexico, 1822-1857*. Durham, 1926.

_____, *Liberalism in Mexico, 1857-1929*. Stanford, 1931.

_____, *Santa Anna, The Story of an Enigma who once was Mexico*. Norman, 1936.

Cambre, Manuel, *La guerra de tres años en el estado de Jalisco. Apuntes para la historia de la reforma*. Guadalajara, 1892.

Carleton, James H., *The Battle of Buena Vista*. New York, 1848.

Corti, Egon Caesar, *Maximilian and Charlotte of Mexico*. 2 vols., New York, 1928.

Cosío Villegas, Daniel, *Historia moderna de México*. 8 vols., Mexico, 1954-1957.

Cuevas, Mariano, *Historia de la nación mexicana*. México, 1940.

Díaz, Porfirio, *Memorias de 1830-1867*. 2 vols., México, 1922.

Duclos-Salinas, Adolfo, *Héroes y caudillos*. St. Louis, 1906.

Evans, Albert S., *Our Sister Republic: A Gala Trip Through Tropical Mexico in 1869-1870*. Hartford, 1870.

Frías y Soto, Hilarión, *Apuntes biograficos del cuidadano — Jesús González Ortega*. México, 1861.

Foster, John W., *Diplomatic Memoirs*. 2 vols., New York, 1909.

Galindo y Galindo, Miguel, *La gran década nacional, o relación histórica de la guerra de reforma, intervención extranjera y gobierno del Archiduque Maximiliano, 1857-1867*. 3 vols., México, 1904-1906.

García, Genero, *Juárez, Refutación a Don Francisco Bulnes*. México, 1904.

García Granados, R., *Historia de México desde la restauración de la república en 1867, hasta la caída de Porfirio Díaz*. México, 1936.

Gibaja y Patrón, Antonio, *Comentario critico, histórico, auténtico*

149

a las revoluciones sociales de México. 5 vols., Mexico, 1926-1935.

González Ortega, Jesús, *The Presidency of Mexico.* New York, 1866.

González Ortega, José, *El golpe de estado de Juárez, rasgos biográficos del general Jesús González Ortega.* México, 1941.

Handbook of Latin American Studies.

Johnson, Richard A., *The Mexican Revolution of Ayutla, 1854-1855.* Rock Island, 1939.

Knapp, Frank A., "The Apocryphal Memoirs of Sebastian Lerdo de Tejada." *HAHR* (February, 1951), 145-151.

———, *The Life of Sebastian Lerdo de Tejada, 1823-1889.* Austin, 1951.

Lempriere, Charles, *Notes in Mexico in 1861 and 1862.* London, 1862.

Lill, Thomas R., *National Debt of Mexico.* New York, 1919.

Magner, James A., *Men of Mexico.* Milwaukee, 1942.

Mateos, José María, *Historia de la masonería en México desde 1806 hasta 1884.* México, 1884.

Mecham, J. Lloyd, *Church and State in Latin America.* Chapel Hill, 1934.

Memorias inéditas del Lic. Don Sebastián Lerdo de Tejada. Brownsville, 1911. (Apocryphal).

Negrete, Doroteo, *La verdad ante la figura militar de Don Miguel Negrete.* Puebla, 1936.

Ocaranza, Fernando, *Juárez y sus amigos.* 2 vols., México, 1930.

Ortega y Pérez Gallardo, Ricardo, *Historia genealógica de las familias mas antiguas de México.* 3 vols., México, 1908-1910.

Owsley, Frank L., *King Cotton Diplomacy. Foreign Relations of the Confederate States of America.* Chicago, 1931.

Parra, Porfirio, *Estudio histórico-sociológico sobre la reforma en México.* Guadalajara, 1906.

Peral, Miguel A., *Diccionario biográfico mexicano.* México, no date.

Pérez Verdía, Luis, *Historia particular del estado de Jalisco.* 3 vols., Guadalajara, 1911.

Planchet, Regis, *La cuestión religiosa en México o sea vida de Benito Juárez.* Rome, 1906.

Portilla, Anselmo de la, *Méjico en 1856 y 1857, gobierno de General Comonfort.* New York, 1858.

Prida Santacilia, Pablo, *Siguiendo la vida de Juárez.* México, 1945.

Prieto Guillermo, *Lecciones de historia patria escritas para los alumnos del colegio militar.* México, 1893.

_____, *Memorias de mis tiempos.* 2 vols., Mexico, 1948.

Riva Palacio, Vicente (ed.), *México a través de los siglos.* Vol. V by José M. Vigil, *La Reforma.* Barcelona, 1889.

Rivera Cambas, Manuel, *Historia de la reforma religiosa política y social en México.* México, 1875.

_____, *Los gobernantes de México.* Mexico, 1873.

Rivera y Sanromán, Agustín, *Anales mexicanos. La reforma y el segundo imperio.* México, 1904.

Robertson, William S., "The Tripartite Treaty of London." *HAHR,* XX (May, 1940), 167-189.

Roeder, Ralph, *Juárez and His Mexico.* 2 vols., New York, 1947.

Salado Álvarez, Victoriano, *Episódios nacionales.* 6 vols., México, 1945.

Scholes, Walter V., "Church and State at the Mexican Constitutional Convention, 1856-1857." *The Americas* (October, 1947), 151-174.

_____, "*El Mensajero* and the Election of 1871 in Mexico." *The Americas* (July, 1948), 61-67.

_____, *Mexican Politics During the Juárez Regime, 1855-1872.* Columbia, Missouri, 1957.

Sheridan, P. H., *Personal Memoirs.* 2 vols., New York, 1888.

Sierra, Justo, *Juárez, su obra y su tiempo.* México, 1905-1906.

Sosa, Francisco, *Las estatuas de la reforma.* México, 1900.

Valdés, Manuel, *Memorias de la guerra de reforma.* México, 1913.

Velázquez, Primo F., *Historia de San Luis Potosí.* 4 vols., México, 1948.

Villaseñor y Villaseñor, A., *Estudios históricos.* 4 vols., México, 1897-1906.

Zamacois, Niceto de, *Historia de Méjico, desde sus tiempos mas remotos hasta nuestros dias.* 18 vols., Barcelona, 1878-1880. With a continuation by Cosmes, Francisco G. 4 vols., Barcelona, 1901-1903.

Zayas Enriquez, Rafael de, *Porfirio Díaz,* New York, 1908.

_____, *Benito Juárez, su vida — su obra.* México, 1906.

Zerecero, Anastasio, *Memorias para la historia de las revoluciones en México.* México, 1869.

Index

Gallegos, Sabino, 15 n. 1
Garcia, Alejandro, 111, 120 n. 25
Garcia Munive, Miguel, 61 n. 20
Garza y Ballesteros, Archibishop
  Lázaro, 50
El Globo de México, 126-127, 129
Gobernación, 59 n. 2
Godoy, José A., 120 n. 25
Gómez, Jesús, 27
Gómez, Manuel Z., 125
Gómez Farías, Benito, 43
Gómez Farías, Valentín, 3, 140 n. 51
González, Manuel, 136
González Ortega, Jesús: accepts
  Juárez' decision not to resign, 85;
  accused of violating word to
  French, 94 n. 8; aid sought against
  Vidaurri, 86; answers Zarco/s
  attacks, 52-53; appointed Secretary
  of War, 49, 50; asks support for
  Cadena, 132; assessment of,
  141-144; assessment of by Cosmes,
  144; birth of, 1; at Borrego,
  69-70; at bullfight, 26; called
  "Devil Preacher," 25; campaigns
  against Conservatives, 54, 58;
  candidate for state legislature, 9;
  center of anti-Juárez activities, 57;
  church attacks on, 27; claims
  presidency, 104; commands
  Division of Zacatecas, 52-53;
  commands division against French,
  84; and Committee of Public
  Safety, 56; Conservative attacks on,
  24-25; coup d'etat of Juárez, 142;
  death of, 135; debate over absence
  from country, 109; defeated by
  Ramírez, 33; defends Constitution
  of 1857, 10; defense of departure
  from Mexico, 104; defense of
  legality, 37, 44, 52, 54, 59, 102,
  125, 128, 132; denies support of
  Cadena, 132; and Doblado, 26; in
  Durango, 27; education of, 1;
  elected to Congress, 123 n. 54,
  132; elected president of Supreme

Court, 68; elected to state
  legislature, 12; and election of
  1871, 133; emphasizes religious
  issue, 24; escape from French, 75;
  espouses liberal philosophy, 11;
  exchanges letters with Forey, 71;
  flees French, 85-86; French views
  on, 114-115; funeral oration to,
  136; as general of armies of
  Center and North, 38; governor of
  Zacatecas, 21-22, 67, 76; held
  responsible for Cruz-Aedo's death,
  31 n. 25; illness of, 42, 138 n. 30;
  imprisonment and release of, 101,
  125, 127, 129; issues 1859 reform
  laws, 25; issues protests against
  Juárez, 102; at Jalatlaco, 55; as jefe
  politico, 7; as Justice of Peace, 1;
  at Las Ánimas, 23; and law
  regarding National Guard, 12-13;
  leaves United States, 101-102;
  legal president, 143, and Sebastián
  Lerdo de Tejada, 134; library of,
  135; love of women, 1; at
  Majoma, 88; as member of council
  of state in Zacatecas, 14; military
  commander of San Luis Potosí, 67;
  as moderado, 10; named
  Commander-in-Chief, 42; named
  interim president of Supreme
  Court, 56; named
  second-in-command to Doblado,
  58; as newspaper editor, 9;
  nominated to state legislature, 132;
  opposes prolonging of Juárez'
  term, 92-93; and pacification plan
  with Castillo, 41-42, 47 n. 45; at
  Peñuelas, 34-35; and Plan of
  Hospicio, 5; poet, 2, 17 n. 21;
  prepares publication against Juarez,
  109; presidential ambitions of 39,
  62 n. 31, 73-74, 92, 133;
  presidential candidate, 1860, 51;
  pressures Juárez for nationalization
  decree, 30 n. 17; Prieto's opinion
  of, 113; and prisoner exchange,

155

35; promoted by Degollado, 45 n. 21; proposed as gubernatorial candidate, 131-132; publishes Reform Laws, 43; at Puebla, 70-75; at Quemada, 76; questions end of presidential term, 1864, 88-89; recognizes Juárez, 22; rejects Degollado's pacification plan, 41; and religious toleration, 26; requests authority to raise funds in United States, 92, 104; requests Juárez' resignation, 84; requests permission to leave Mexico, 90; resigns command against Conservatives, 58; resigns as president of supreme court and interim president of nation, 131; resigns as Secretary of War, 50, 52; returns to Mexico, 115-116; restored to rank of general, 135; in retirement, 134-136; at San Miguel Calpulalpan, 43; secretary to Méndez Mora, 16 n. 19; seeks agreement with French, 69; seeks support of United States, 113; seizes Zacatecas, 27; sends circular to foreign ministers in Mexico City, 38; at Silao, 37; speech to congress, 56; split with Juárez, 53; substitute deputy from Zacatecas to constitutional convention, 8; sued by Colonel Allen, 92; support for against Juárez, 99-100, 108 n. 22; supported for presidency, 56; supporters in United States, 114; takes Aguascalientes, 33; takes Mexico City, 43; trip to United States, 91; at Valparaiso, 23; victory parade, 44; at Villa Nombre de Dios, 27 /
González Ortega, Joaquín, 90
González Ortega, José de Jesús, 15 n. 1
González Ortega, Laurito, 96 n. 33, 134
Governorship of Zacatecas, 76

Grant, General U. S., 116
Great Britain, *conducta* seized, 40; funds belonging to subjects taken, 23; relations with Mexico, 65; and Treaty of London, 66; views on forcing Juárez out, 62 n. 36; Zamacona-Wyke agreement, 66
Guadalajara, city of, 23, 38, 42-43, 85; seminary of, 1
Guadalupe, Zacatecas, 25
Guanajuato, city of, 76, 85; state of, 14, 23
El Guardia Nacional, 12
Guerrero, state of, 6, 14, 87
Guerrero, B. D. Rafael, 15 n. 1
Haro y Tamariz, Antonio de, 16 n. 16
Hidalgo y Esnaurrizar, José Manuel, 65
Hinojosa, Pedro, 77 n. 5
History of the Protestant Reform, 135
History of Religion, 135
Horace, 135
Hospicio, plan of, 4, 5
Hoyo, Benito and Ignacia del, 15 n. 1
Huatusco, Veracruz, 76
Huerta, Epitacio, 104, 108 n. 22
Ibarra Ramos, Francisco, 108 n. 22
La Iberia, 75
Iglesias, José María, 81 n. 48; Secretary of Justice, 17 n. 23; Secretary of Treasury, 114
Imprisonment of González Ortega, 127, 129, 142; congressional investigation of, 127; continues as issue after release, 130-131; criticisms of Juárez for, 126-127; judicial investigation ordered, 126; protests against, 125
Inquiries Concerning the Truth, 135
Jalapa, Mexico, 76
Jalatlaco, battle of, 55
Jalisco, battle of, 22; state of, 14, 83, 133

156

resignation, 94 n. 7; attacked at Quemada, 76; circumstances of death, 138 n. 28; escapes from French, 75; held responsible for Cruz-Aedo's death, 31 n. 25; killed, 130; opposes Vidaurri, 86
Paulson, Captain John, 115
Pavón, Francisco G., 7
Paz, Francisco, 108 n. 22
Paz, Ireneo, 139 n. 44
Peace negotiations, 69
Peñuelas, Aguascalientes, 34, 142
Periódico Oficial, 100
Philadelphia, Pennsylvania, 125
El Pobre Diablo, 9, 60 n. 15
Political clubs, 53
Political parties, 2-4, 12
Presidential election of 1857, 9-12, *passim;* of 1860, 51, 55; of 1861, 55; of 1867, 117-118; of 1871, 133-134
Presidential term, expiration of Juárez', 92-93, 99; of Juárez prolonged, 101; of Juárez questioned, 88-89; Lerdo's plan for extension of, 96 n. 29; of Santa Anna, 5-6; support for Juárez' extension of, 106
Prieto, Guillermo, 4, 10, 100; defends González Ortega, 105, 109, 126; enemy of Sebastián Lerdo de Tejada, 120 n. 29; escapes from French, 75; exchange with Juárez over González Ortega's absence, 100; opinions of Juárez and González Ortega, 113; opposes Juárez, 99; rumored seeking return to Juárez fold, 121 n. 31; as Secretary of Treasury, 18 n. 32, 50, 52
Prisoner release, 35, 37
Protests, 102
Puebla, city of, 74, 106; siege of, 68, 70-72, 74-75, 80 n. 42, 105; state of, 14, 103, 142
Puros, 9, 18 n. 31

Quemada, hacienda of, in San Luis Potosí, 76
Querétaro, city of, 38, 85, 106, 117; state of, 14
Quiroga, Julián, 23
Ramírez, Ignacio, 50
Ramírez, Silverio, 33, 34, 45 n. 10
Reform laws, of 1859, 24; of 1833, 3; González Ortega's part in, 143; as part of general program, 30 n. 16; published at end of war, 43
Regules, Nicolás de, 121 n. 25
Rivera, Aureliano, 130-131
Robert, Cipriano, 108 n. 22, 110
Rocha, Juan N., 26
Rocha y Portu, Pablo, 108 n. 22
Roeder, Ralph, cited, 99
Román, Juan F., 9, 12, 17 n. 28
Romero, Matías, 92, 93, 99; attacked by González Ortega, 117; given official defense of Juárez, 105; pays González Ortega's court debts, 102; possible resignation, 107 n. 3; received González Ortega in United States, 91; replies to González Ortega's petition, 127-128; reports on González Ortega's actions in United States, 91; suggests reply by Juárez, 110
Rosa, Luciano de la, 28
Rubi, Domingo, 120 n. 25
Ruiz, Joaquín, 77 n. 3
Ruiz, Manuel, 100, 104, 114
Sacred Books of the Orient, 135
Sain Alto, Zacatecas, 86
Saint Thomas, 135
Salamanca, Guanajuato, 21
Salazar, Mexico, 54
Saligny, Count de, 65, 69, 83
Salinas, San Luis Potosí, 33, 36
Saltillo, Coahuila, 85, 117, 125, 131
San Antonjo, Texas, 102, 126
San Joaquín, Zacatecas, 117
San José de García, Veracruz, 75
San Juan de Teúl, Zacatecas, 1, 2, 5,

159

10, 42
San Lorenzo, Puebla, 74
San Luis, Plan of, 139 n. 44
San Luis Potosí, city of, 23, 75, 85, 87; state of, 14, 67, 83, 105, 133
San Mateo Valparaíso, Zacatecas, 1
San Miguel Allende, Guanajuato, 85
San Miguel Calpulalpan, Tlaxcala, 43
San Pedro, Guadalajara, 41
Sánchez Ochoa, Gaspar, 108 n. 22, 113
Sánchez Román, José M., 27, 33
Santa Anna, Antonio López de, 4, 5-6
Santacilia, Pedro, 91, 92, 105, 106
Sedgwick, General Thomas D., 116
Seizure of Guanajuato treasury, 23
Separation of powers, 50
Serrano, F. de P., cited, 59
Seward, Secretary William H., 112, 115
Sheridan, General Phillip H., 115, 116
Sierra, Justo, cited, 34-35, 42
El Siglo Diez y Nueve, 49, 53, 59
Silao, Guanajuato, 21, 37, 142
Sinaloa, state of, 87
Smith, Congressman Green Clay, 111
Sombrerete, Zacatecas, 86
Sonora, state of, 87
La Sombra de García, 9, 12; advice regarding political parties, 11-12; on agriculture, 17 n. 28; supports Comonfort, 9
Spain, 65, 67; and Treaty of London, 66
Summa Theologica, 135
Summary of Ecclesiastical History, 135
Tehuacan, Puebla, 70
Le Temps, 75
Terán, Jesús, 77 n. 5
Tezuitlan, Puebla, 76
Theological Institutions, 135
Tlaltenango, Zacatecas, 5, 7, 16 n.

19, 22; elects González Ortega to congress, 124 n. 54; to state legislature, 132
Tlaxcala, state of, 14
Tocqueville, Alexis de, 125
Togno, Colonel Juan, 73, 90
Toluca, México, 43
Tonila, Colima, 26
Tovar, Pantaleón, 110
Treaty of London, 66
Treviño, Gerónimo, 136
United States, 62 n. 6; holds González Ortega, 115-116; intervention by, 128, 143; war with, 3
Uraga, General José López, 84, 93 n. 4; and Committee of Public Safety, 56; defeated at Guadalajara, 37; joins González Ortega, 33; at Loma Alta, 34; and prisoner exchange, 35
Valparaíso, Zacatecas, 23
Vega, Plácido, 110
Veracruz, city of, 24, 33, 106; state of, 14
Veuillot, author of Library of Religion, 135
Vicario, Santiago, 108 n. 22
Vidaurri, Santiago, 36, 86-87; Juárez' doubts about, 94 n. 11; pressures for nationalization decree, 30 n. 17; refuses revenues, 86; urges Juárez' resignation, 94 n. 10
Viesca, A. S., 120 n. 25
Vigil, José María, cited, 74
Villa Nombre de Dios, Durango, 27
Villalobos, Joaquín, 109, 111
Villanueva, district of, 9, 12
Virgil, 135
War of the Reform, 14, 21; brutality of, 24; end of, 43; fall of 1860, 36-40; military events leading toward end of, 43; number of Conservative victories, 28 n. 1; religious aspects, 24
War with the United States, 3

160